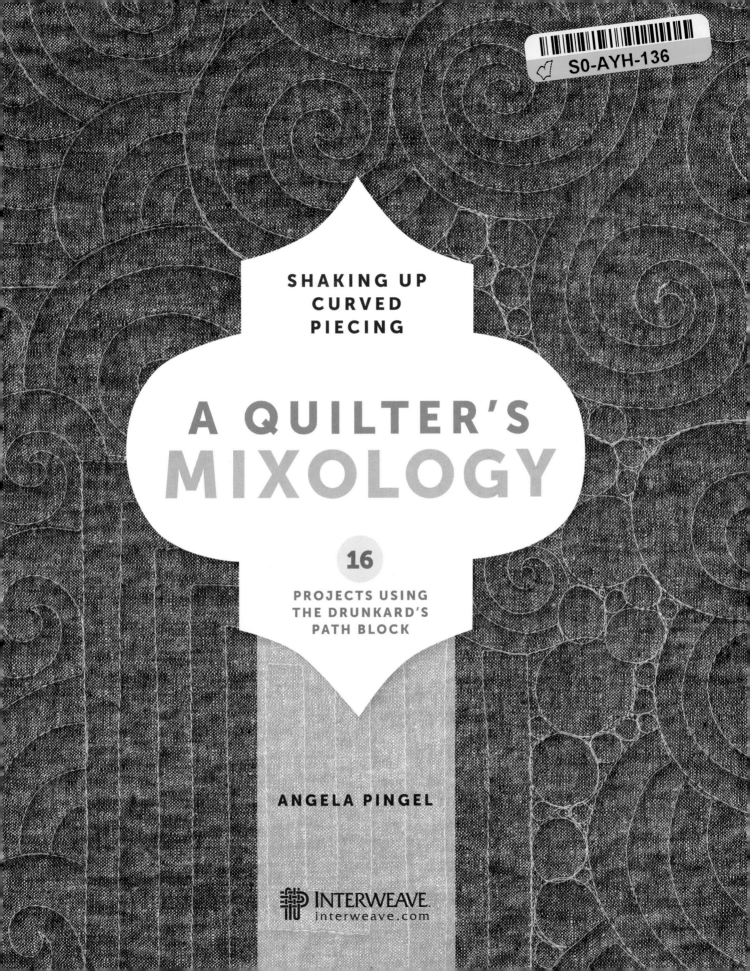

SHAKING UP
CURVED
PIECING

A QUILTER'S
MIXOLOGY

16

PROJECTS USING
THE DRUNKARD'S
PATH BLOCK

ANGELA PINGEL

INTERWEAVE.
interweave.com

EDITOR *cynthia bix*

TECHNICAL EDITOR *linda turner griepentrog*

PHOTOGRAPHER *joe hancock*

ILLUSTRATOR *missy shepler*

STYLIST *allie liebgott*

ASSOCIATE ART DIRECTOR *julia boyles*

COVER AND INTERIOR DESIGN *karla baker*

PRODUCTION DESIGNER *katherine jackson*

 Interweave
A division of F+W Media, Inc.
4868 Innovation Drive
Fort Collins, CO 80525
interweave.com

Manufactured in China by RR Donnelley Shenzhen

Library of Congress Cataloging-in-Publication Data

Pingel, Angela.
 A quilter's mixology : shaking up curved piecing / Angela
Pingel.
    pages cm
 Includes index.
 ISBN 978-1-62033-122-4 (pbk.)
 ISBN 978-1-62033-123-1 (PDF)
 1. Patchwork--Patterns. 2. Quilting--Patterns.
 3. Patchwork quilts. I. Title.
 TT835.P5623 2014
 746.46--dc23
                    2013038542

10 9 8 7 6 5 4 3 2 1

DEDICATION

to my brother Thaddeus:

You were one of the first people to support my love
of quilting and fabric. There are not too many brothers who
would happily take a quilt to college that was made by their sister.
And it was not just any quilt. It was a Suspender Sam and Sunbonnet Sue
sampler quilt. I couldn't have picked a less masculine pattern. But you were
unfazed by the design and informed me that you would simply use the quilt
to help you meet girls. You knew they would be impressed by anyone who
loved his sister so much. Oh, silly guy. I'm so sorry I was never able to find
out if that technique for impressing girls would have worked. I think it
was pretty brilliant on your part, and it is one of
my favorite memories of you.

You are missed every day.

ACKNOWLEDGEMENTS

No project of this scale is the work of just one person. I would like to gratefully acknowledge the generosity and support of all of those who helped make my vision a reality.

TO MY HUSBAND, MICHAEL:

It goes without saying that none of this would have been possible without your endless support. You have helped me to accomplish a dream and kept me sane when the process was less than dreamlike. To simply say thank you is not enough, but it is a start. Thank you, my dear, for all that you do for me and for our family.

TO MY QG GIRLS:

I'm not sure how this collection of souls found each other, but I'm grateful every day for you ladies. Thank you for holding my hand, pushing me forward, and always being my biggest cheerleaders.

TO THE INTERWEAVE TEAM:

I continue to be thankful for the many, many people who have contributed to making this book. From the book proposal to the photo shoot, editors upon editors, and every single assistant, you have all helped to create my dream.

I would also like to thank the following people and companies:

AccuQuilt and Sizzix. Many thanks for the use of your die cutting machines. Your companies are helping change the scope of the quilting world with each pass through the cutter.

Robert Kaufman Fabrics, Birch Fabrics, Michael Miller Fabrics, Art Gallery Fabrics, Moda Fabrics, Cloud9 Fabrics, Oakshott Fabrics, Dear Stella Fabrics, and **Free Spirit Fabrics.** Thank you for supplying me with yards and yards of material to make so many of the projects in this book. I love your fabrics and your willingness to invest in authors.

Aurifil. Thank you, Alex, for your overwhelming generosity and supply of wonderful thread (and for your everentertaining posts on Facebook).

Pellon. Thank you for the amazing supply of batting and pillow forms. Working with each batting type was a wonderful journey to take with this book.

Fiskars. I'm so thankful for the many notions you supplied me with, from cutting mats to scissors. My world is much crisper and cleaner as a result.

Sandra, of **Just Curves** and the **Curve Master Presser Foot.** You have already trail blazed the path for making sewing curves easier and fun. I love your quarter-circle templates especially.

And last, but most definitely not least, thank you to quilter Krista Withers (kristawithersquilting.blogspot.com). You are an artist, and I'm privileged to have your work grace some of my quilts here in this book. Your ability to understand what I want and then create something even better never fails to amaze me. I dream of a world where you can quilt all of my quilts!

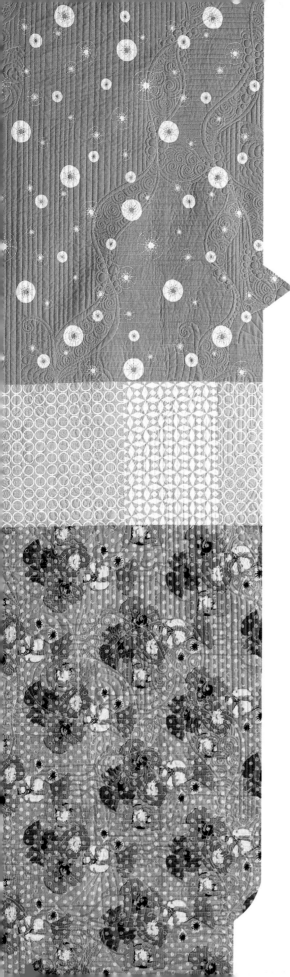

CONTENTS

A WALK DOWN
DRUNKARD'S PATH

This book explores the possibilities of quilt design with quarter-circle curves. My own path to quilting started back in my childhood, when I began sewing because I wanted to make myself a dress. I continued to sew garments through my teens and then discovered the world of quilting. Now, I've become especially intrigued with the possibilities of curved piecing.

The block I chose to explore is a traditional favorite, the Drunkard's Path, which is one of the most versatile blocks available to quiltmakers. It has been a popular choice for well over a hundred years.

The block's name describes its basic design, which suggests the weaving walk of a drunkard staggering homeward. This block was used during the late 1800s and early 1900s by the Women's Christian Temperance Union (WCTU) to express disapproval of alcohol and its use. Such quilts were often made in the WCTU colors of blue and white, which symbolized purity.

However, symbolism aside, Drunkard's Path is an intriguing design in its own right. It has been and continues to be a favorite, because it is such an amazingly versatile block.

The classic Drunkard's Path block is made up of pieces that are quarter circles drafted on squares. You put the pieces together by sewing a concave curve to a convex curve. These blocks can be arranged in many different ways. The classic Drunkard's Path setting is shown on the facing page. Different settings can be created simply by rotating the blocks and by playing with the placement

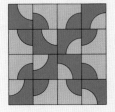

clockwise from top left **CLASSIC DRUNKARD'S PATH BLOCK, DEVIL'S PUZZLE BLOCK, DRUNKARD'S PATH QUILT, LOVE RING QUILT**

of dark- and light-value fabrics. Although the traditional pattern uses just two colors—one dark and one light—the look can be greatly changed by using multiple colors. There have been lots of variations of the block over the years. Traditional variations and settings have gone by names such as Crooked Road, Devil's Puzzle, Love Ring, Wanderer's Path, and Wonder of the World.

When I decided to work with this block, my challenge was to use it in a way that honored its deep, tra-ditional roots and yet also took it to a new place. There is beauty in the original pattern that intrigued me and made me look at the shapes more closely. What exactly were the limitations of this block? In the end, there seemed to be few, and literally hundreds of ideas came to me. The trick became to fine-tune these into usable and appealing quilt designs that could be shared.

When the quarter-circle shape is broken down and taken apart, it can be turned into something entirely new.

It becomes a modern and graphic design that reflects the original block but introduces a new vision for using the shape. Some of the designs in this book share elements with traditional variations, while others take off in another direction to create something entirely new.

Taking a tongue-in-cheek approach to the block's original name, I thought of modern mixology—the art and craft of mixing drinks. Take a little of this, a little of that, and combine them in a new way with a dash of creativity. The result is something fresh, novel, and delectable. That's what I've concocted with these projects.

above MEDALLION BABY QUILT
(PAGE 62) IS BASED ON
THE TRADITIONAL LOVE RING DESIGN.

opposite LOOSELY CURVED WALL
HANGING (PAGE 92) IS A FRESH,
UPDATED TAKE ON CURVED PIECING.

FEARLESS CURVED PIECING

The Drunkard's Path block *does* require curved piecing. As a former garment sewer, I have never been daunted by sewing curves. However, if you're new to it, never fear. In these pages, I'll show you my method for sewing curves with ease. I'll also explain how to cut curved pieces using either an acrylic curve template, the templates provided in this book, or the newer, super-fast die-cutters. You'll be a pro in no time!

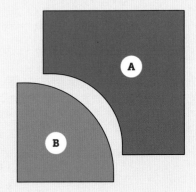

This block is made from two basic pieces: a square and a quarter-circle. The square (**A**) has a concave curve, and the circle (**B**) has a convex curve. When sewn together with a ¼" (6 mm) seam allowance, these pieces become a perfect square.

note Before they are sewn, the curves have different diameters, which can be disconcerting when you first look at your templates! But don't worry—they are supposed to be different. They each have a seam allowance added to them. It will all turn out perfectly when you sew them together.

FINISHED BLOCKS

traditional block

modern block

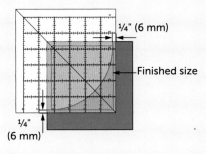

¼" (6 mm)

Finished size

¼"
(6 mm)

trimmed block

There are two types of blocks you'll be using in this book—the "traditional," or classic, Drunkard's Path block, and what I call the "modern" Drunkard's Path block. The latter has a skinny leg on the L-shaped piece and a wider quarter circle.

To help make stitching easier when joining the modern-style A and B pieces, the L-shaped pieces are cut slightly *oversized*. (The quarter-circle portions are cut *to size*.) After sewing and pressing the curve, trim to the unfinished block size needed for the project. It's a little extra effort, but you'll find it's more accurate this way.

CUTTING CURVED PIECES

I cut curved pieces from fabric in one of two ways—using templates with a rotary cutter or using a die-cutting machine. The die-cutters are great time savers if you have dies the right size as described on pages 12–13. (Some, but not all, of my patterns are compatible with die-cutters). Paper or acrylic templates can be used in every situation.

When cutting pieces, always place the straight edge either crosswise or lengthwise on the fabric's straight of grain. This results in a bias curved area, perfect for easing to the opposite curve.

TEMPLATES

The template patterns for the projects in this book can be found on the pattern insert at the back of this book. Many of the projects use the same size templates to make finished Drunkard's Path units that measure either 3½" × 3½" (9 × 9 cm), 4" × 4" (10 × 10 cm), or 7" × 7" (18 × 18 cm). So you can actually use one set to cut out multiple projects. Other projects have special larger or smaller template sizes.

Use your favorite method to transfer the template patterns onto paper or template plastic. This lightweight plastic is available at most quilting stores and online. You can cut it with scissors, a rotary cutter, or a craft knife. It makes durable templates that you can use repeatedly.

Purchased acrylic curve templates like those shown in the photo on page 12 can be used as alternatives to the paper template patterns in this book. Such templates are available online at sites such as Just Curves (www.justcurves.biz). You could also have some Plexiglas templates custom cut at a local plastics shop.

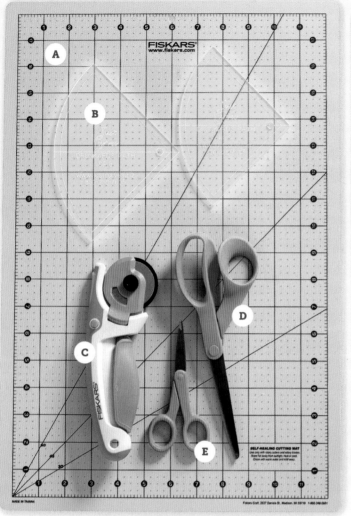

essential tools

Shown here is a standard selection of tools for the modern quilter. If you don't already have these, consider adding them to your personal collection. Get the highest quality you can afford. Basics are fine. You don't need a lot of "bells and whistles," but reliable tools are the first step to successful quilting.

Although the sizes of your see-through acrylic rulers are a personal choice, I would recommend two sizes—6" × 24" (15 × 61 cm) and 3" × 18" (7.5 × 45.5 cm)—plus a small square ruler 6" × 6" (15 × 15 cm) for trimming units or blocks.

For more about the acrylic curve templates, see Cutting Curved Pieces (page 11).

A CUTTING MAT

B ACRYLIC CURVE TEMPLATES

C ROTARY CUTTER

D SEWING SHEARS

E TRIMMING SCISSORS

F ACRYLIC RULER

DIE-CUTTERS

You can neatly cut curved pieces from fabric using templates. But there is another way that's even easier. The die-cutters that have burst onto the quilting scene give all of our hands a break from laboriously cutting intricate and odd-shaped pieces. Cutting a large number of template-based blocks is quick work with the help of these ingenious little machines designed for home use.

Throughout this book, I make use of two different companies' die-cutters and Drunkard's Path dies—AccuQuilt and Sizzix. Because they offer different size dies from each other, I was able to make use of the varying sizes to create multiple design options.

Both die-cutters operate on the same basic concept. You place your fabric on a cutting pad over your chosen die, which has inlaid "blades" protected with foam (to keep your fingers safe). Then, you crank the handle of the machine, and the machine's roller provides even pressure to push the pad through and cut the fabric. You can cut multiple layers of fabric at once. Follow the manufacturer's instructions for your particular machine, and it will cut out your fabric shapes accurately every time.

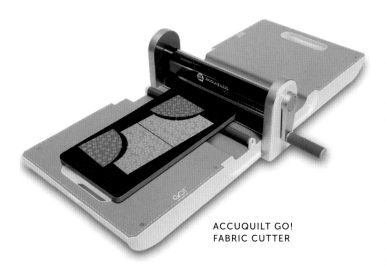

ACCUQUILT GO!
FABRIC CUTTER

SIZZIX BIG SHOT MACHINE

AccuQuilt offers two sizes of die-cutters. The larger size AccuQuilt GO! Fabric Cutter uses a die that makes a 7" × 7" (18 × 18 cm) finished Drunkard's Path unit. The smaller, more compact GO! Baby Fabric Cutter uses a die that makes a 3½" × 3½" (9 × 9 cm) finished Drunkard's Path unit. Both cut two of each template piece needed to make one Drunkard's Path unit. AccuQuilt dies provide a center notch on each piece for easy matching. Both cutters fold up to optimize space.

Sizzix has a single Drunkard's Path die that makes a 4" × 4" (10 × 10 cm) finished unit. The die comes in two separate pieces for the block—one for the con-

vex curve piece and one for the concave curve piece. This is especially helpful when you have an uneven number of the curves per fabric. The Sizzix die does not have a center notch mark. I prefer to use the Sizzix cutter when cutting from 5" × 5" (12.5 × 12.5 cm) charm squares, because it wastes very little fabric.

HOW TO CUT

With both templates and die-cutters, first cut your fabric into strips at the width specified in the project pattern. If the pattern is die-cutter-compatible, I call for strips cut at a generous width for ease of use with the die-cutter. If the pattern is intended for template use only, the width of the strip is listed at an exact dimension for the template. (If using templates for the die-cutter-compatible patterns, you will find that you have a bit of extra fabric in the width for the template. Simply cut from the strip, trimming any excess fabric away. Or cut squares the height of the strip, and cut your templates from the squares.)

When using templates, I first cut strips of fabric to the desired width. Then I cut each strip into squares. Finally, I lay the appropriate template on each square and cut around it. Unless you are fussy-cutting fabric to spotlight a particular motif, you can cut multiple pieces at once using a template. (Be sure your rotary cutter blade is sharp!) I find that I can easily cut two or three layers of fabric around a template shape without distortion.

If you are using a die-cutter, simply fold the cut strip neatly over the die, back and forth multiple times, to get as many pieces as possible from one pass through the cutter.

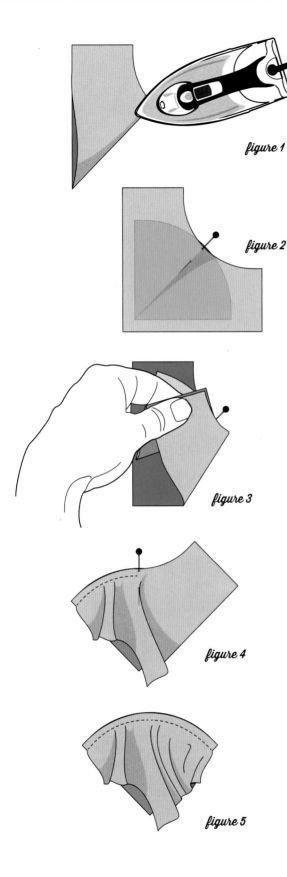

figure 1

figure 2

figure 3

figure 4

figure 5

SEWING CURVES

In this section, I present my tried-and-true method for sewing curves, as well as some alternative methods.

note Sewing traditional and modern blocks is done the same way; the only difference is in the trimming at the end of the sewing process.

MY METHOD

I tried a number of options before I landed on the method that works best for me when sewing curves. I wanted to sew the two pieces together quickly but most importantly, accurately. It did me no good to sew the curves at top speed and then end up getting out the seam ripper to correct mistakes because I wasn't able to be precise enough. Likewise, I didn't have the luxury of sewing at a snail's pace. I've sewed hundreds, perhaps thousands, of curves, so I'm pretty confident that you will like my method.

STITCHING

1 Mark the center of each piece along the curved edge (both convex and concave). To do this, simply fold the piece in half and give it a quick press just at the curved edge (**fig. 1**). Then use one—yes, just one—pin to pin the convex and concave pieces together at the center, right sides together (**fig. 2**).

note If you use the AccuQuilt die-cutter, it marks the center for you. But if you are using acrylic templates or the Sizzix die-cutter, you will need to mark the center yourself.

2 Sew the pieces together in two steps. First, align the two pieces together along one straight edge of each (**fig. 3**), and sew from that edge to the pin at the center, easing the two pieces together (**fig. 4**).

3 Stop, trim your threads, and then repeat from the opposite side (**fig. 5**).

The trick is to ignore the fact that you are stitching a curve. Pretend it is a straight seam. Mind over matter can really help you sew a curve. And truly, when the diameter of the curve is large, you practically *are* sewing a straight line. Make sure that the section of the seam where the needle is piercing the fabric always has the ¼" (6 mm) seam allowance, and "forget" about the rest.

I find that this method gives me really clean ends to my quarter-circle curves, which is very helpful for the patterns that require precision. And I like sewing along the same outer curve the whole time. I can stay in one frame of mind while sewing. Plus, sewing to the middle each time gives me a chance to double check my first seam allowance when sewing the second half. No one is perfect, and sometimes a bit of re-sewing is necessary.

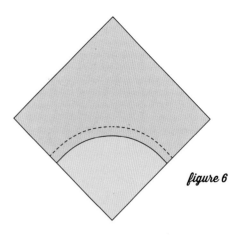

figure 6

PRESSING

An important part of sewing curved pieces together is proper pressing. Contrary to popular belief, there is no need to clip the curves. The ¼" (6 mm) seam allowance is slight and presses cleanly to either side of the seam.

I most often choose to press the seam allowance toward the inner curve because of the trimming and disappearing seams I use in many patterns throughout this book **(fig. 6)**.

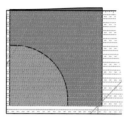

figure 7

1 Press the block first from the wrong side, gently pulling the smaller corner curve away from the seam. Press from the center and then on each end. As you press, do not put too much stress on this seam, because you can easily distort the square.

2 Flip the piece over and re-press the curve from the right side, double-checking that the fabric is pulled flat but not taut.

3 Finish up your quarter-circle block by trimming it with a rotary cutter as necessary. Curved blocks can easily get pulled out of square, so trimming is often necessary to square up the block. Using your ruler, square up your block to the desired size **(fig. 7)**.

mistakes happen!

Sewing curves quickly and simply is definitely doable, but some mishaps can occur. Here are three of the most common problems and the solutions for fixing them.

To prevent stretching in the first place, be gentler with your handling of the curved pieces. Since the curve on both pieces exposes the bias of the fabric, the pieces are vulnerable to stretching. This can happen when cutting, sewing, or pressing, or a combination of all three. Try to determine at what point in the process you are putting the most stress on the bias. Also note that some fabrics are more easily stretched than others, even though you are using the same technique to sew them. Some can make you feel like a rock star seamstress, and others make you want to throw in the towel.

PROBLEM #1

When sewing the curve, you end up with a tuck in your fabric. The fabric has bunched in one or more places and overlapped **(fig. 1)**.

SOLUTION

Make friends with your seam ripper. Tucks in the seam allowance of a curved piece are actually a very easy fix. Use your trusty seam ripper to rip out just a few small stitches over the offending tuck. Then take out one stitch on either side. Now you can easily stretch the fabric smooth **(fig. 2)**. Re-stitch the seam in place.

PROBLEM #2

The ends of the curves do not align properly. One of them stretched, and the curve is uneven **(fig. 3)**.

SOLUTION

The fabric is not evenly eased throughout the curved seam. Seam ripper time again. Your best bet is ripping out the entire seam and starting again, carefully pinning the fabric together. Depending on where the ease went off, you might be able to partially rip the seam and re-sew it.

PROBLEM #3

Your finished block is obviously out of square **(fig. 4)**.

SOLUTION

If it isn't too far off square, simply trim your block back into shape, as described in Step 3 of Pressing (page 15).

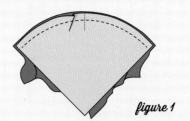

figure 1

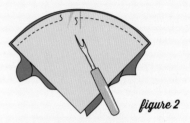

figure 2

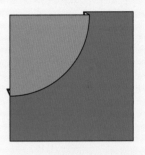

figure 3

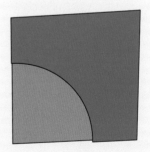

figure 4

ALTERNATIVE METHODS

I know that we all see different ways to tackle the same job, and what works best for me may not be your favorite method. So I'll mention some alternatives, and you can experiment with what method is best for you. Bottom line: Use the method that gets you the results you want. There is no one right way to sew these pieces together.

One popular method for sewing curved pieces together is to pin the pieces at multiple points along the entire curve, then sew continuously from one end to the other (see below). I put this in the category of always accurate, but slow. It's the method I started with when sewing curves, and it's a reliable way to do it.

You might also try using just three pins—one at the middle and one on each end—and then sewing continuously from one end to the other (shown below). I like this method for speed, and I find it fairly comparable to my method (although you don't get that chance to double check your seams).

A lot of people swear by the no-pin method. They match up the two pieces and as they sew, they ease the fabric together with their hands along the entire seam from one end to the other. Some also use a special foot, such as the Curve Master Presser Foot. This foot is designed to sew curves with no pins; the foot automatically eases the concave and convex pieces together as you sew. The no-pin method is a great method if you can do it. I personally find it difficult to get the ends to finish accurately, and I find it hard to evenly ease the fabric together without the help of the marked center.

PUTTING BLOCKS TOGETHER

I use a technique that I call "disappearing seams" to join two modern Drunkard's Path blocks. Each modern Drunkard's Path block is trimmed down to a square with a ¼" (6 mm) seam allowance left on the L-shaped piece's outer edges.

When two of these blocks are sewn together, the outer ¼" (6 mm) seams literally disappear. You are left with only the smooth curves meeting perfectly together at each end.

Correct pressing is essential to creating smooth, disappearing seams. You will need to press the seam allowance toward the inner curve. This reduces the bulk of sewing together two blocks with a ¼" (6 mm) seam allowance. If you pressed the seams toward the outer curve, then you would have six layers of fabric, rather than two, to sew through at the seam.

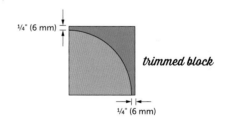

trimmed block

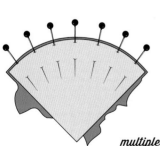

multiple-pin method

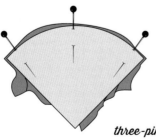

three-pin method

disappearing seams

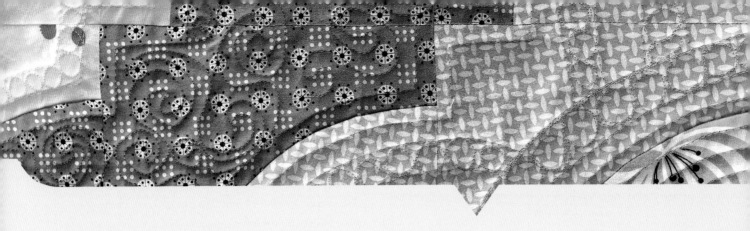

THOUGHTS ON COLOR + FABRIC

Selecting the fabrics for any project is always a favorite moment in the design process for me. I have what I fondly refer to as a "fabric addiction," which essentially means that I really like fabric: I like to see it, own it, touch it, and use it. There are so many options for fabric designs these days that I would challenge any person in the world not to find a fabric they adore. Like most quilters, I prefer to work with quality, 100 percent cotton fabrics.

above DETAIL FROM MEDALLION BABY QUILT (PAGE 62)

FABRIC DESIGNS

Sewing curves adds a whole new dimension to selecting fabrics for a quilt design. Cutting curved pieces from fabric patterns gives you a unique opportunity to use directional prints as well as overall patterns. They also lend themselves to fussy-cutting—selecting particular elements in the fabric design to focus on. Directional prints in particular can be your best friend (or your worst enemy) when sewing quarter-circle curves, because you may have to pay attention to four different orientations of a single fabric. But they can be a spectacular showpiece in a quilt as well, providing extra interest simply with the choice of the right fabric.

When choosing prints, consider their scale. Are the fabric patterns large-, medium-, or small-scale? There is no hard-and-fast rule for scale selection, but it should never be ignored. My personal preference is to use a mix of scales in a single quilt pattern, such as in *Nine Patch Curves* (page 84). But sometimes a pattern can be

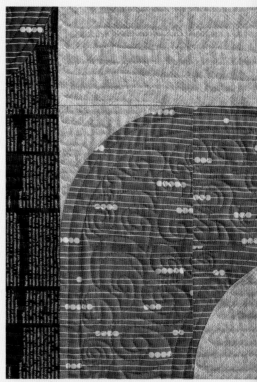

above DIRECTIONAL FABRICS IN TELEPORT QUILT (PAGE 72)

left FUSSY-CUT FABRIC IN NINE PATCH CURVES QUILT (PAGE 84)

very specifically geared toward using a particular print of one scale, repeated in several colors as in *Paint Drips* (page 98). Very large-scale prints can yield some interesting results when cut into small pieces for a quilt, as in *Ornamental* (page 114). Small-scale prints can often read as a solid fabric in a sea of larger-scale prints.

A mixture of visual textures is also important to any design scheme. The uber-popular text prints look great mixed with modern florals. Or mix a stripe, a reproduction print, a polka dot, and a solid. As with color selection, the right mix of print textures is a personal choice. A quilt may be perfect in all dot prints or all stripes. But most often, a healthy balance of many options will provide the most interest as well as cohesion to your design.

And of course, don't forget to think about incorporating solid fabrics or crossweaves into your fabric selection. (Crossweaves are fabrics like shot cottons and chambrays, which are woven with different colors in the warp and weft so they have special coloration.)

above LARGE-SCALE PRINTS ADD INTEREST WHEN CUT IN SMALL PIECES AS FOR ORNAMENTAL QUILT (PAGE 114).

right SMALL-SCALE PRINTS READ AS SOLIDS IN PAINT DRIPS QUILT (PAGE 98).

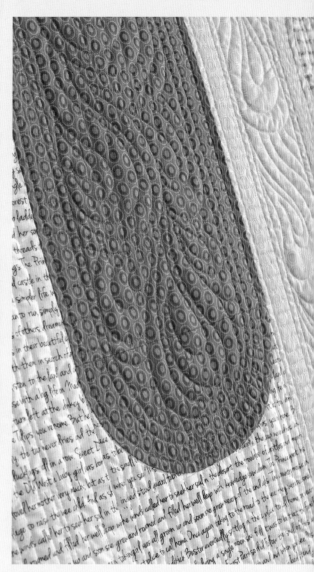

Prints are so exciting and constantly changing that it can be easy to overlook the value of creating with all solids or even interspersing solids throughout your project. But solids really are a vital aspect of good fabric selection. They can act as a neutral, providing a resting place for your eyes. Or they can have the opposite effect, acting as a powerful pop of bold color.

Woven solids have no right or wrong side to the fabric, which makes them enormously versatile and easy to use, especially when working with curves. Be careful when working with them, though, because solids also don't hide anything. So your sewing may need to be a bit more precise when working with them.

Consider using a solid or printed "blender" fabric as one of your basics. It can help bridge the gaps between colors and fabrics to create harmony overall. Fabrics go in and out of style, so keep your eye out for blenders with a modern aesthetic.

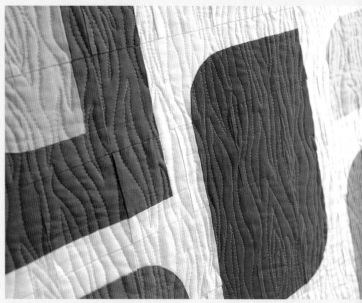

above IN LOOSELY CURVED WALL HANGING (PAGE 92), SOLIDS LEND BIG, BOLD IMPACT.

left THE YELLOW BACKGROUND PRINT ACTS AS A BLENDER FABRIC IN MOD GARDEN LAP QUILT (PAGE 106).

below A MIX OF PRINT TEXTURES, INCLUDING TEXT PRINTS, PROVIDES VISUAL INTEREST IN NINE PATCH CURVES QUILT (PAGE 84).

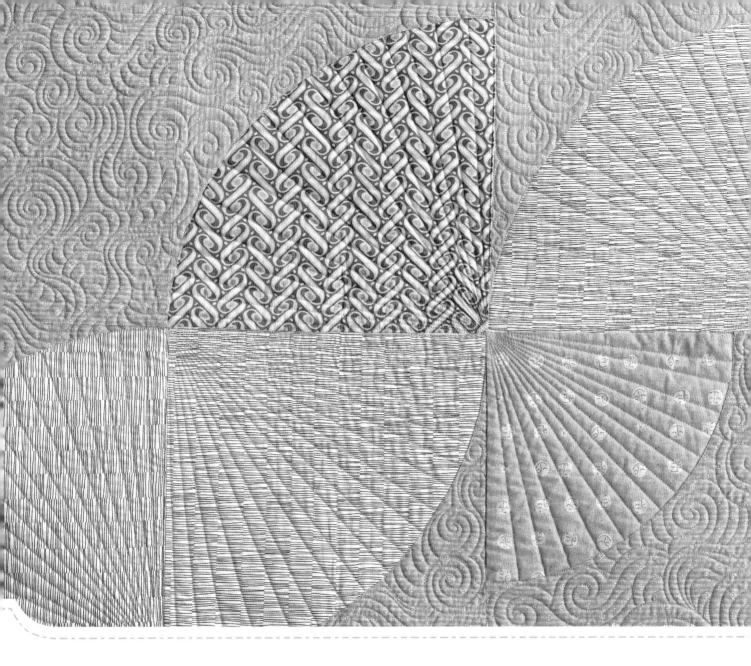

COLOR

Add color into the mix, and you have a whole other set of design decisions to make. Color is the cherry on top of the fabric choices. A good design is essential to any fabric; a great color is a bonus. For me, fabric selection starts with a fabric whose pattern and color make my heart go pitter-patter. That special fabric that cries out to me, just begging me to use it. I think of it as the focal fabric. The right focal fabric gives you a place to build your whole color palette for a project. I select the rest of my fabrics to coordinate with, but not necessarily match, that initial focal print. Interestingly, that focal fabric may never make it into the final project, or it may be the backing for a project. But even so, it has provided inspiration.

A great palette for a quilt is anything that you love. That may seem like a cop-out on giving you instructions for selecting fabrics, but I truly believe that if you love a selection of fabrics, then you will love your finished project. Any mix of colors can work when you find the right focal print or quilt design to pull them all

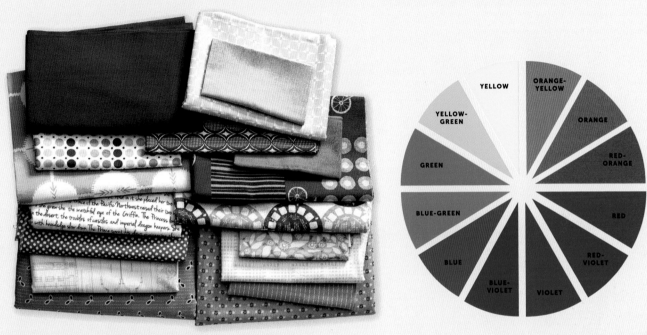

above **TYPICAL SELECTION OF COORDINATING FABRICS**

right **SIMPLE COLOR WHEEL**

opposite **BLUE AND ORANGE IN ORANGE TWIST QUILT (PAGE 28) ARE GREAT COMPLEMENTARY COLORS.**

together. That said, there are some points to take into consideration when selecting a complete set of fabrics for a project.

Study a color wheel to help you gain an understanding of how colors relate to each other. There are entire books written by experts on color theory, and I would do this topic an injustice by trying to summarize it in this book. However, I will touch here on a few of the most basic color schemes.

On the simplest level, there are three types of colors—primary (red, yellow, and blue), secondary (green, orange, and purple), and tertiary (colors such as blue-green or orange-yellow that are mixes of a primary and secondary color). To achieve color harmony, you can use a number of different color schemes. The simplest is the complementary color scheme—two colors, such as red and green, that are across from each other on the color wheel. Others include harmonizing schemes (two colors side-by-side on the wheel) and analogous schemes (three adjacent colors). Any number of color schemes can work for a quilt—even a whole rainbow. More than likely, you naturally gravitate toward one type of color scheme and

are not even aware of it. I personally tend to love complementary colors because of the high contrast they provide.

Although color schemes provide great guidelines, try to keep your palette from being too coordinated. Color schemes are most interesting when there is a pop of a color that is a bit unexpected, like the dark gray flower petals in *Flower Power* (page 34). I know that I have a good selection of fabrics when there is a fabric that rubs me the wrong way! The best way to avoid the pitfalls of overly coordinated color schemes is to pull your fabric selections from a variety of designers' fabric lines.

Don't forget neutrals. They can help ease together any number of colors. I rarely make a project without a neutral somewhere in the quilt. I love color, so sometimes it can be hard to select a "non color" as one of the fabrics in my project. But they always help balance the dynamic colors that I choose first. A neutral fabric gives your eyes a place to rest in the dance of colors and patterns—an essential moment in any design. Neutrals can be as obvious as a white or cream, or a less obvious navy, soft blue, black, or gray. Any fabric that lets your eyes rest is a neutral in your palette.

right THREAD COLORS ARE ALMOST UNLIMITED, AS SHOWN IN THIS DEPENDABLE THREAD FROM AURIFIL.

opposite THE DARKER PETALS ADD PUNCH IN FLOWER POWER QUILT (PAGE 34).

A WORD ABOUT THREAD

When working with cotton fabrics, as I do, I most often piece with cotton thread that matches my fabric. I'll admit that I've been known to use whatever I have around that is the right color, or, out of laziness, even what is already in the machine. But, do as I say and not as I do!

As with all tools and supplies, it is worth getting the best quality thread that you can afford. You will put a lot of work into making a quilt, and you don't want to make the process harder on yourself by using thread that constantly breaks as you are sewing. (If that is happening, by the way, check your needle—it might be too dull!)

I piece with a stitch length on the smaller side— somewhere between 2.2 and 2.5 mm on my machine settings. This eliminates the need for backstitching at either end of a seam. Cotton thread works well for this because it will cling to your fabric a little more, holding those ends close together.

When I am quilting the backing, batting, and quilt top, I am a bit looser with my thread choices.

It all depends on what I want to accomplish with my quilting. Do I want clear, straight-line quilting? Then I will probably use a heavier-weight cotton thread. Do I want to do free-motion machine quilting with a lot of movement? Then most likely I choose a polyester thread. For decorative stitches that have a bit of shine, I almost always use a rayon thread. When handstitching, as I do for my bindings, I tend to use whatever color I have that matches. I do enjoy using a 50-weight cotton thread for that, if I have a choice.

Take all of these suggestions with a grain of salt. There are a lot of different threads out there, and each machine seems to prefer a different kind. I have two domestic machines that I use constantly, and I get different results from each with the same thread. Experiment to find the thread that you prefer to have on hand and the weight you prefer for particular types of sewing.

A **MIX** OF PROJECTS

In this section are sixteen projects that are based on Drunkard's Path blocks. Add a wealth of prints and solids, colors, blocks, and layouts, and then mix, blend, and shake them up to make some wonderful quilted concoctions. Make a small pillow or a big, full-size quilt, a piece of wall art or something for a new baby's crib. Follow the color schemes shown in the photos, or be your own mixologist and create something entirely new!

note Some of the projects share template patterns, while others have their own unique template patterns. Many use both shared and unique patterns. (Three of the shared templates have corresponding AccuQuilt or Sizzix dies, should you choose to use those instead of templates.) Each template pattern has a designated letter (A, B, C, and so on). Pay careful attention that you are using the correct ones for your chosen project. Template patterns are on the insert at the back of this book.

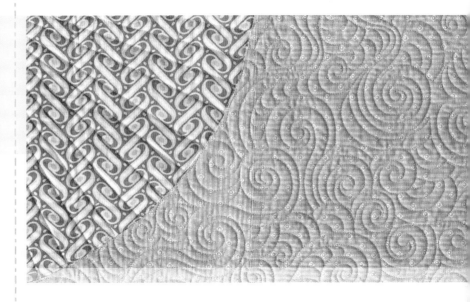

finished size
74" × 98" (188 × 250 cm)

designed and pieced by
ANGELA PINGEL

quilted by
KRISTA WITHERS

MATERIALS

Fabric amounts are based on yardage with a usable width of 42" (106.5 cm). Fat quarters are 18" × 22" (45.5 × 56 cm).

2½ yd (2.3 m) neutral print fabric

10 assorted orange print fat quarters

4¼ yd (4 m) aqua print fabric

6 yd (5.5 m) backing fabric

¾ yd (68.5 cm) binding fabric

82" × 106" (208 × 269 cm) batting

TOOLS

Template patterns I, J, U, and V

Template plastic or paper

CUTTING

WOF = width of fabric

FROM NEUTRAL PRINT FABRIC:
- Cut 7 strips 12½" (31.5 cm) × WOF. Cut 19 pieces V from the strips.

FROM THE ORANGE PRINT FAT QUARTERS:
- Cut 10 pieces J and 9 pieces V.

FROM AQUA PRINT FABRIC:
- Cut 12 strips 12½" (31.5 cm) × WOF. From these, cut the following:
  » From 4 strips, cut 10 squares 12½" × 12½" (31.5 × 31.5 cm).
  » From 3 strips, cut 9 pieces I.
  » From 5 strips, cut 28 pieces U.

FROM BACKING FABRIC:
- Cut 2 rectangles 106" (269 cm) × WOF.

FROM BINDING FABRIC:
- Cut 9 strips 2½" (6.5 cm) × WOF.

the pattern

ORANGE
TWIST
QUILT

the mix

Swirls of color garnished with bright slices of orange

With the help of large blocks, this quilt goes together surprisingly quickly. Perhaps the curves at this scale require more pins, but they are ultimately easier to sew due to their gentle radius. A great feature of this quilt design is its flexibility: It looks equally good no matter how you orient it. Every time I look at it, I see vanilla ice cream twisting into a cone from an old-fashioned soft-serve ice cream machine. Create your own flavor and savor how delicious it is!

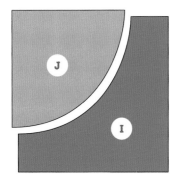
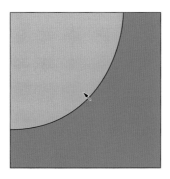

figure 1

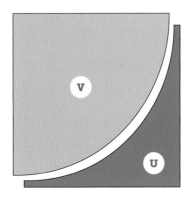
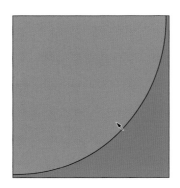
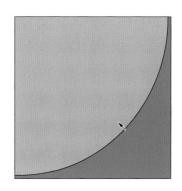

figure 2

MAKING THE BLOCKS

Unfinished block size: 12½" × 12½" (31.5 × 31.5 cm)
This quilt has forty-eight blocks.

1   Sew together ten aqua pieces I, and ten orange pieces J **(fig. 1)**. Press the seams toward piece J. You will have a total of ten quarter-circle blocks 12½" × 12½" (31.5 × 31. 5 cm).

2   Sew together nineteen aqua print pieces U and nineteen neutral print pieces V **(fig. 2)**. Sew together nine aqua print pieces U and nine orange print pieces V. Press all the seams toward piece V. You will have a total of twenty-eight quarter-circle blocks 12½" × 12½" (31.5 × 31.5 cm).

MAKING THE QUILT TOP

1   Refer to the Orange Twist Construction Diagram (page 32) to lay out the quilt top into eight rows of six blocks each. Use the pieced blocks plus the ten unpieced aqua blocks. Pay careful attention to the orientation and placement of the blocks.

2   Sew together each row. Press all seams open. Sew the eight rows together to complete the quilt top. Press all seams in one direction.

FINISHING

1. Refer to Finishing Your Quilt (page 132) or use your favorite methods to layer and baste the quilt top, batting, and backing.

2. Quilt as desired. On a longarm machine, quilter Krista Withers quilted radiating lines on the neutral and orange "fans" and a beautiful pattern of swirls on the aqua background.

3. Bind your quilt using my French double-fold binding method as described in Binding (page 139) or your own preferred method.

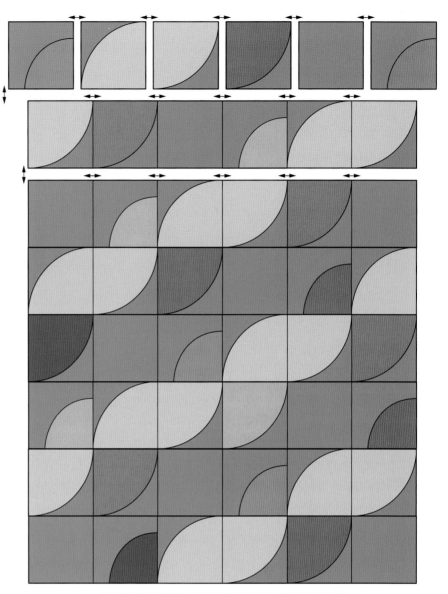

ORANGE TWIST CONSTRUCTION DIAGRAM

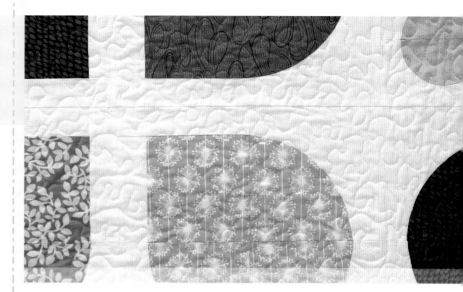

finished size
70" × 84" (178 × 213 cm)

designed, pieced, and quilted by
ANGELA PINGEL

MATERIALS

Fabric amounts are based on yardage with a usable width of 42" (106.5 cm). Fat quarters are 18" × 22" (45.5 × 56 cm).

1 yd (91.5 cm) dark gray print fabric

1 yd (91.5 cm) aqua print fabric

1 yd (91.5 cm) green print fabric

1 yd (91.5 cm) pink print fabric

1 fat quarter light gray solid fabric

1 fat quarter aqua solid fabric

1 fat quarter green solid fabric

1 fat quarter orange solid fabric

4¼ yd (4 m) white solid fabric

5⅛ yd (4.7 m) backing fabric

⅔ yd (61 cm) binding fabric

78" × 92" (198 × 234 cm) batting

TOOLS

Template patterns A, B, E, and F or 3½" (9 cm) and 7" (18 cm) AccuQuilt dies and cutter (page 13)

Template plastic or paper (if using patterns)

CUTTING

WOF = width of fabric

FROM DARK GRAY PRINT FABRIC:
- Cut 3 strips 6½" (16.5 cm) × WOF. Cut 18 pieces F from the strips.
- Cut 1 strip 6" (15 cm) × WOF. Cut 6 squares 6" × 6" (15 × 15 cm).

FROM AQUA PRINT FABRIC:
- Cut 3 strips 6½" (16.5 cm) × WOF. Cut 18 pieces F from the strips.
- Cut 1 strip 6" (15 cm) × WOF. Cut 6 squares 6" × 6" (15 × 15 cm).

FROM GREEN PRINT FABRIC:
- Cut 3 strips 6½" (16.5 cm) × WOF. Cut 18 pieces F from the strips.
- Cut 1 strip 6" (15 cm) × WOF. Cut 6 squares 6" × 6" (15 × 15 cm).

continued on the next page >

the pattern

FLOWER
POWER
QUILT

the mix

Mix and match 1960s-style flowers in two sizes and punch them up with a bright fizz of color.

Come join the movement with this Flower Power quilt. A fresh, updated version of times long gone by, this modular pattern plays on two sizes of flowers. The two combine in an offset pattern that keeps your eye moving. Pull out your AccuQuilt cutter and both die sizes for this one, and you will have your fabric cut in no time!

FROM PINK PRINT FABRIC:
- Cut 3 strips 6½" (16.5 cm) × WOF. Cut 18 pieces F from the strips.
- Cut 1 strip 6" (15 cm) × WOF. Cut 6 squares 6" × 6" (15 × 15 cm).

FROM LIGHT GRAY SOLID FABRIC:
- Cut 5 strips 3½" × 18" (9 × 45.5 cm). Cut 18 pieces B from the strips.
- Cut 1 strip 3" × 18" (7.5 × 45.5 cm). Cut 6 squares 3" × 3" (7.5 × 7.5 cm).

FROM AQUA SOLID FABRIC:
- Cut 5 strips 3½" × 18" (9 × 45.5 cm). Cut 18 pieces B from the strips.
- Cut 1 strip 3" × 18" (7.5 × 45.5 cm). Cut 6 squares 3" × 3" (7.5 × 7.5 cm).

FROM GREEN SOLID FABRIC:
- Cut 5 strips 3½" × 18" (9 × 45.5 cm). Cut 18 pieces B from the strips.
- Cut 1 strip 3" × 18" (7.5 × 45.5 cm). Cut 6 squares 3" × 3" (7.5 × 7.5 cm).

FROM ORANGE SOLID FABRIC:
- Cut 5 strips 3½" × 18" (9 × 45.5 cm). Cut 18 pieces B from the strips.
- Cut 1 strip 3" × 18" (7.5 × 45.5 cm). Cut 6 squares 3" × 3" (7.5 × 7.5 cm).

FROM WHITE SOLID FABRIC:
- Cut 1 strip 6" (15 cm) × WOF. Cut the strip into 18 strips 2" × 6" (5 × 15 cm).
- Cut 1 strip 7½" (19 cm) × WOF. Cut the strip into 18 strips 2" × 7½" (5 × 19 cm).
- Cut 1 strip 4" (10 cm) × WOF. Cut the strip into 18 strips 1½" × 4" (3.8 × 10 cm).
- Cut 1 strip 3" (7.5 cm) × WOF. Cut the strip into 18 strips 1½" × 3" (3.8 × 7.5 cm).
- Cut 15 strips 8½" (21.5 cm) × WOF. Cut the strips into 72 squares 8½" × 8½" (21.5 × 21.5 cm). Cut 1 piece E from each square. Use the large scrap pieces left from cutting pieces E to cut 72 pieces A.

FROM BACKING FABRIC:
- Cut 2 rectangles 92" (234 cm) × WOF.

FROM BINDING FABRIC:
- Cut 8 strips 2½" (6.5 cm) × WOF.

MAKING THE BLOCKS

This quilt has twenty-four small petal blocks and twenty-four large petal blocks, each of which is a quarter of the flower patterning. All of the blocks are constructed in the same manner.

SMALL PETAL BLOCKS (FOUR PETALS TOGETHER)

Unfinished block size: 14½" × 14½" (37 × 37 cm) Make six.

1 Sew together curved pieces A and B **(fig. 1)** as follows:

- Sew 18 white solid pieces A to 18 light gray solid pieces B.
- Sew 18 white solid pieces A to 18 aqua solid pieces B.
- Sew 18 white solid pieces A to 18 green solid pieces B.
- Sew 18 white solid pieces A to 18 orange print pieces B.

Press the seams toward piece B. You will have a total of seventy-two quarter-circle units.

2 Sew a white solid strip 1½" × 3" (3.8 × 7.5 cm) to the bottom of a solid color square 3" × 3" (7.5 × 7.5 cm). Press the seam toward the square. Sew a white solid strip 1½" × 4" (3.8 × 10 cm) to the left side. Press the seam toward the white solid strip **(fig. 2)**. Make six units with a light gray solid square, six with an aqua solid square, six with a green solid square, and six with an orange solid square.

3 Sew together the quarter-circle units from Step 1 to make six matching pairs in each color **(fig. 3)**. Press all seams open. You have six quarter-circle units unused.

4 Sew the remaining six quarter-circle units from Step 1 to the matching units from Step 2 **(fig. 4)**. Press all seams open.

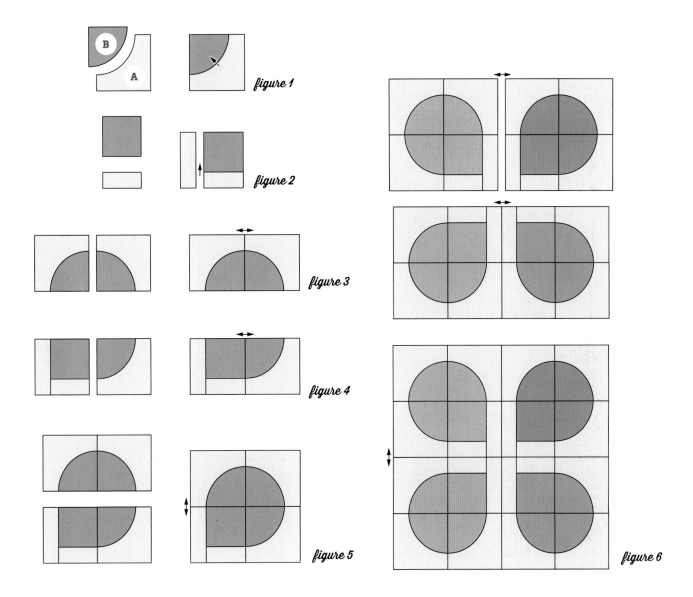

figure 1

figure 2

figure 3

figure 4

figure 5

figure 6

5 Assemble the units of matching colors from steps 3 and 4, aligning center points **(fig. 5)**. You will have six white/light gray units, six white/aqua units, six white/green units, and six white/orange units. Press all seams open.

6 To complete the small petal blocks, assemble the units from Step 5, matching seams in the center **(fig. 6)**. Sew each orange unit to an aqua unit, and each green unit to a light gray unit. Press the seams open. Then sew each orange/aqua unit to a green/light gray unit to form the small petal block. Press the seams open. Square up the blocks to 14½" × 14½" (37 × 37 cm).

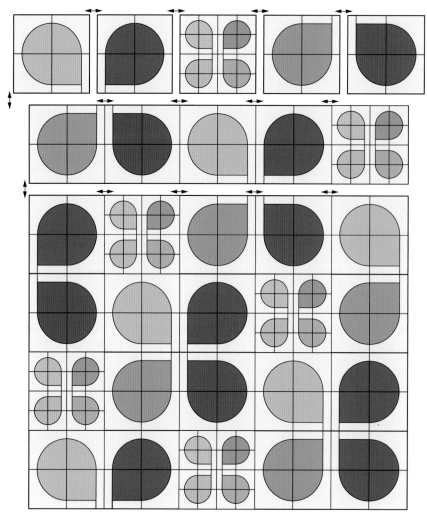

FLOWER POWER CONSTRUCTION DIAGRAM

- -

LARGE PETAL BLOCKS (SINGLE PETAL)

Unfinished block size: 14½" × 14½" (37 × 37 cm)
Make twenty-four.

Follow the same basic directions as in steps 1 through 5 for the small petal blocks.

1 Sew together curved pieces E and F as follows:

- Sew 18 white solid pieces E to 18 dark gray print pieces F.

- Sew 18 white solid pieces E to 18 aqua print pieces F.

- Sew 18 white solid pieces E to 18 green print pieces F.

- Sew 18 white solid pieces E to 18 pink print pieces F.

Press the seams toward piece F. You will have a total of seventy-two quarter-circle units.

2 Sew a white solid strip 2" × 6" (5 × 15 cm) to the bottom of a color print square 6" × 6" (15 × 15 cm). Press the seam toward the square. Sew a white solid strip 2" × 7½" (5 × 19 cm) to the left side. Press the seam toward the white solid strip. Make six units with a dark gray print square, six units with an aqua print square, six units with a green print square, and six units with a pink print square.

3 Sew together the quarter-circle units from Step 1 to make twenty-four matching pairs. Press all seams open. You will have twenty-four quarter-circle units unused.

4 Sew the remaining quarter-circle units from Step 1 to the matching units from Step 2. Press all seams open.

5 To complete the large petal blocks, assemble the units of matching colors from steps 3 and 4, matching seams in the center. Press all seams open. You will have six dark gray print/white solid blocks, six aqua print/white solid blocks, six green print/white solid blocks, and six pink print/white solid blocks. Trim the blocks to 14½" × 14½" (37 × 37 cm).

MAKING THE QUILT TOP

1 Refer to the Flower Power Construction Diagram to sew together the quilt top in six rows of five blocks each, aligning adjacent seams. Press all seams open.

2 Sew the rows together aligning adjacent seams to complete the quilt top. Press all seams in one direction.

FINISHING

1 Refer to Finishing Your Quilt (page 132) or use your favorite methods to layer and baste the quilt top, batting, and backing.

2 Quilt as desired. I quilted an allover meandering pattern that adds texture to the quilt top.

3 Bind your quilt using my French double-fold binding method as described in Binding (page 139) or your own preferred method.

the pattern

PAIR OF
PILLOWS

the mix

Variations on a theme, created in two different patterns, in multiple shades of blue

Pillow projects let you dip your toes into the water of curved piecing without getting soaked. Here are two classically based designs that use traditional Drunkard's Path layouts. As a pair, these pillows are striking when made in coordinating color schemes. Both pillows use the same number of units, but the result is amazingly different. The projects give you just a taste of the versatility of the quarter-circle unit and how it can be manipulated to yield a myriad of patterns.

Both pillows are constructed the same way, with pieced and quilted tops, a full lining, zippered back, and binding. They give you an opportunity to try out many of the methods that you will use for larger projects, but on a much smaller scale.

Remember, don't be afraid to change up the color schemes and make these patterns your own.

finished size
19½" × 19½" (49.5 x 49.5 cm)

designed, pieced, and quilted by
ANGELA PINGEL

MATERIALS

Fabric amounts are based on yardage with a usable width of 42" (106.5 cm).

½ yd (45.5 cm) white solid fabric

1 fat quarter aqua solid fabric

1 fat quarter blue solid fabric

1 fat quarter dark blue print border fabric

1 yd (91.5 cm) lining fabric

⅓ yd (30.5 cm) backing fabric

3½" × 20" (9 × 51 cm) fabric strip for zipper placket cover

¼ yd (23 cm) binding fabric

20" (51 cm) zipper

¼" wide (6 mm) paper-backed fusible web tape

24" × 24" (61 × 61 cm) batting

20" × 20" (51 × 51 cm) pillow form

TOOLS

Template patterns A and B or 3½" (9 cm) AccuQuilt die and cutter (page 13)

Template plastic or paper (if using patterns)

Zipper foot

CUTTING

WOF = width of fabric

FROM WHITE SOLID FABRIC:
- Cut 2 strips 4½" (11.5 cm) × WOF. Cut 13 pieces A from the strips.
- Cut 2 strips 4" (10 cm) × WOF. Cut 12 pieces B from the strips.

FROM AQUA SOLID FABRIC:
- Cut 4 strips 4" × 22" (10 × 56 cm). Cut 13 pieces B from the strips.

FROM BLUE SOLID FABRIC:
- Cut 3 strips 4½" × 22" (11.5 × 56 cm). Cut 12 pieces A from the strips.

FROM DARK BLUE PRINT BORDER FABRIC:
- Cut 4 strips 2" × 22" (5 × 56 cm).

continued on the next page >

TEMPLE
PILLOW

The pattern for this pillow is particularly effective when made with solid fabrics, as shown. But you could spice things up by replacing one of the solids with a print. Give this pillow a try when you are comfortable with the idea of curved piecing but just want a small project to tackle.

MAKING THE BLOCKS

Unfinished block size: 4" × 4" (10 × 10 cm)
This pillow top has twenty-five blocks.

1 Sew each white piece A to an aqua piece B **(fig. 1)**.

2 Sew each blue piece A to a white piece B **(fig. 2)**. Press all seams toward the B piece. You will have a total of twenty-five quarter-circle blocks. Trim the blocks to 4" × 4" (10 × 10 cm) square.

MAKING THE PILLOW TOP

1 Arrange the blocks in five rows of five blocks each, as shown in the Temple Pillow Construction Diagram, alternating colors and block orientation as shown.

2 Sew the blocks together into rows, matching adjacent seams. Press the seams open.

3 Sew the rows together, matching adjacent seams. Press the seams in one direction.

4 Trim two of the border strips to 2" × 18" (5 × 45.5 cm) and the other two to 2" × 21" (5 × 53.5 cm). Sew the shorter strips to opposite sides of the pillow. Press the seams toward the border. Sew the longer strips to the remaining sides of the pillow. Press the seams toward the border.

5 Baste the pillow top to the batting. Using your favorite method, quilt as desired. I quilted simple fan lines and handstitched accents on the blue areas, outlines on the aqua curves, and left the white areas unquilted. Trim the pillow top to 20" × 20" (51 × 51 cm) square.

6 Follow the instructions for Constructing the Pillows (page 46) to finish your pillow.

figure 1

figure 2

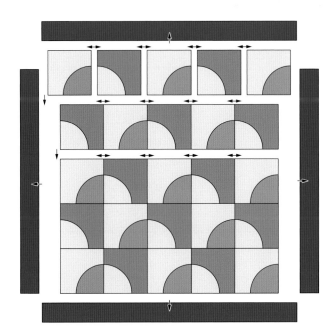

TEMPLE PILLOW CONSTRUCTION DIAGRAM

finished size
19½" × 19½" (49.5 × 49.5 cm)

designed, pieced, and quilted by
ANGELA PINGEL

MATERIALS

Fabric amounts are based on yardage with a usable width of 42" (106.5 cm).

⅝ yd (57 cm) white solid fabric

1 fat quarter *each* of 5 gradated shades of blue solid fabric*

1 fat quarter dark blue print border fabric

1 yd (91.5 cm) lining fabric

⅓ yd (30.5 cm) backing fabric

3½" × 20" (9 × 51 cm) fabric strip for zipper placket cover

¼ yd (23 cm) binding fabric

20" (51 cm) zipper

¼" (6 mm) wide paper-backed fusible web tape

24" × 24" (61 × 61 cm) batting

20" × 20" (51 × 51 cm) pillow form

*These will be referred to as blue fabrics 1 through 5, with 1 the lightest, and 5 the darkest.

TOOLS

Template patterns A and B or 3½" (9 cm) AccuQuilt die and cutter (page 13)

Template plastic or paper (if using patterns)

Zipper foot

CUTTING

WOF = width of fabric

FROM WHITE SOLID FABRIC:
- Cut 4 strips 4½" (11.5 cm) × WOF. Cut 25 pieces A from the strips.

FROM BLUE FABRIC 1:
- Cut 1 strip 4" × 22" (10 × 56 cm). Cut 1 piece B from the strip.

FROM BLUE FABRIC 2:
- Cut 2 strips 4" × 22" (10 × 56 cm). Cut 5 pieces B from the strips.

FROM BLUE FABRIC 3:
- Cut 3 strips 4" × 22" (10 × 56 cm). Cut 9 pieces B from the strips.

continued on the next page >

OMBRÉ PILLOW

This pillow is the very traditional Drunkard's Path pattern but with an updated twist. It makes use of an ombré pattern, in which a color gradates from light to dark. Use your imagination and envision this in other monochromatic colors or even a rainbow. This is the perfect beginner project: It's a manageable size, and there are no curves to match.

FROM BLUE FABRIC 4:
- Cut 2 strips 4" × 22" (10 × 56 cm). Cut 7 pieces B from the strips.

FROM BLUE FABRIC 5:
- Cut 1 strip 4" × 22" (10 × 56 cm). Cut 3 pieces B from the strip.

FROM DARK BLUE PRINT BORDER FABRIC:
- Cut 4 strips 2" × 22" (5 × 56 cm).

FROM LINING FABRIC:
- Cut 1 square 20" × 20" (51 × 51 cm) and 2 pieces 10½" × 20" (26.5 × 51 cm).

FROM BACKING FABRIC:
- Cut 2 rectangles 10½" × 20" (26.5 × 51 cm).

FROM BINDING FABRIC:
- Cut 3 strips 2½" (6.5 cm) × WOF.

MAKING THE BLOCKS

Unfinished block size: 4" × 4" (10 × 10 cm)
This pillow top has twenty-five blocks.

Sew each white piece A to a blue or aqua piece B **(fig. 3)**. Press all seams toward the B piece. You will have a total of twenty-five quarter-circle blocks. Trim the blocks to 4" × 4" (10 × 10 cm) square.

MAKING THE PILLOW TOP

1 Arrange the blocks in five rows of five blocks each, as shown in the Ombré Pillow Construction Diagram. Note the block orientation and color positioning so the blue blocks go from the lightest at the bottom left to the darkest at the top right.

2 Sew the blocks together into rows, matching adjacent seams. Press the seams, alternating directions for each row.

3 Sew the rows together, matching adjacent seams. Press the seams in one direction.

4 Trim two of the border strips to 2" × 18" (5 × 45.5 cm) and the other two to 2" × 21" (5 × 53.5 cm). Sew the shorter strips to opposite sides of the pillow. Press the seams toward the border. Sew the longer strips to the remaining sides of the pillow, and press the seams toward the border.

5 Baste the pillow top to the batting, and use your favorite method to quilt as desired. I quilted fan lines on the blue pieces and hand quilted the white curves with large stitches. Trim the pillow top to 20" × 20" (51 × 51 cm) square.

6 Follow the instructions for Constructing the Pillows (page 46) to finish your pillow.

figure 3

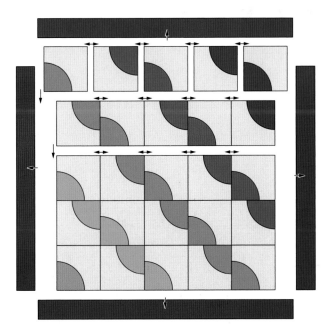

OMBRÉ PILLOW CONSTRUCTION DIAGRAM

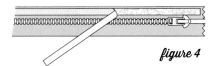

figure 4

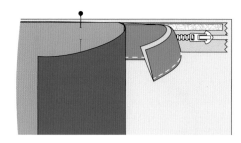

figure 6

figure 5

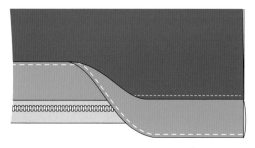

figure 7

CONSTRUCTING THE PILLOWS

1 Baste the 20" × 20" (51 × 51 cm) lining fabric to the batting side of the pillow top. Sew the fabric in place using a scant ¼" (6 mm) seam around the perimeter of the pillow. Set the top aside.

2 Fold the zipper placket fabric in half lengthwise with *wrong* sides together, and press. Topstitch along the folded edge.

3 Following the manufacturer's directions, use your iron to fuse the paper-backed fusible web to one side of the zipper, along the length **(fig. 4)**.

4 Peel off the paper from the fusible, and fuse the folded zipper placket along the length of the zipper, matching the raw edges of the fabric to the upper long edge of the zipper **(fig. 5)**.

5 Place the layers of the pillow back together along the 20" (51 cm) length as follows. Lay one of the 10½" × 20" (26.5 × 51 cm) lining pieces right side up, the zipper teeth up (with placket attached), and one of the 10½" × 20" (26.5 × 51 cm) backing pieces right side down **(fig. 6)**. Pin the layers together.

6 Attach a zipper foot to your sewing machine, and stitch along the zipper, moving the zipper pull as necessary. Fold the fabric and placket seam allowances away from the zipper and topstitch in place **(fig. 7)**.

7 Repeat steps 5 and 6 to complete the other side of the pillow back and lining. (Note that there is no placket in this step.)

8 Trim the pillow back, zipper, and lining to 20" × 20" (51 × 51 cm) square if necessary.

9 Layer the pillow back and pillow top, wrong sides together. Baste around the pillow perimeter.

10 Follow the steps described in Binding (page 139) to sew the binding strips together, and sew the binding to the perimeter of the pillow to finish all the edges.

11 Stuff your pillow with a square 20" × 20" (51 × 51 cm) pillow form, and zip it closed.

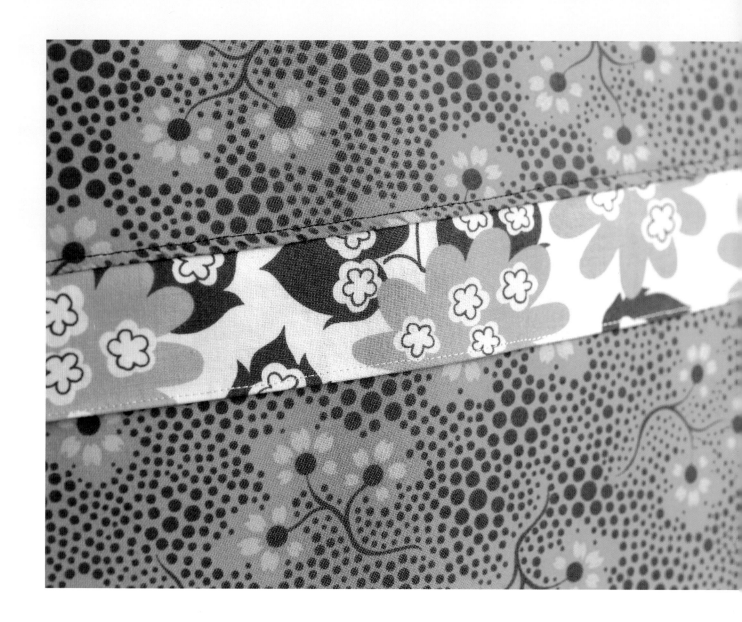

finished size
67" × 90" (170 × 229 cm)

designed, pieced, and quilted by
ANGELA PINGEL

MATERIALS

Fabric amounts are based on yardage with a usable width of 42" (106.5 cm).

1 fat quarter gray print fabric

1 fat quarter orange print fabric

1 fat quarter fuchsia print fabric

1 fat quarter blue print fabric

1½ yd (137 cm) yellow stripe fabric

3⅛ yd (2.9 m) medium green solid fabric

⅞ yd (80 cm) light green print fabric

1⅜ yd (125.5 cm) white solid fabric

2¼ yd (2 m) charcoal solid fabric

5½ yd (5 m) backing fabric

¾ yd (68.5 cm) binding fabric

75" × 98" (191 × 250 cm) batting

TOOLS

Template patterns A and B and/or 3½" (9 cm) AccuQuilt die and cutter (page 13), and template patterns G and H

Template plastic or paper (if using patterns)

CUTTING

WOF = width of fabric

FROM GRAY PRINT FABRIC:
- Cut 3 strips 4" × 22" (10 × 56 cm). Cut 12 pieces B from the strips.

FROM ORANGE PRINT FABRIC:
- Cut 3 strips 4" × 22" (10 × 56 cm). Cut 12 pieces B from the strips.

FROM FUCHSIA PRINT FABRIC:
- Cut 3 strips 4" × 22" (10 × 56 cm). Cut 12 pieces B from the strips.

FROM BLUE PRINT FABRIC:
- Cut 3 strips 4" × 22" (10 × 56 cm). Cut 12 pieces B from the strips.

continued on the next page >

the pattern

TENNIS
MATCH
QUILT

the mix

An unusual combination of traditional and modern quarter-circle blocks, creatively mixed with Log Cabin techniques

Put a spin on the classic Log Cabin design. The offset centers of the blocks give movement and interest to this quilt. A simple twist of one block is all it takes to create motion and send the ball bouncing in all directions. The result of mixing quarter-circle units using Log Cabin techniques is a pleasing balance of strips and curves that is a perfect match.

FROM YELLOW STRIPE FABRIC:

- Cut 19 strips 2½" (6.5 cm) × WOF. From these, cut the following:
  - » From 4 strips, cut 3 strips 2½" × 9½" (6.5 × 24 cm) and 1 strip 2½" × 13½" (6.5 x 34.5 cm) for a total of 12 strips 2½" × 9½" (6.5 × 24 cm) and 4 strips 2½" × 13½" (6.5 x 34.5 cm).
  - » From 12 strips, cut 2 strips 2½" × 11½" (6.5 × 29 cm) for a total of 24 strips and 1 strip 2½" × 9½" (6.5 × 24 cm) for a total of 12 strips.
  - » From the remaining 3 strips, cut 8 more strips 2½" × 13½" (6.5 × 34.5 cm), for a total of 12.

FROM MEDIUM GREEN SOLID FABRIC:

- Cut 24 strips 4½" (11.5 cm) × WOF. Cut 48 strips 4½" x 13½" (11.5 × 34.5 cm) from the strips.

FROM LIGHT GREEN PRINT FABRIC:

- Cut 6 strips 4½" (11.5 cm) × WOF. Cut 48 pieces H from the strips.

FROM WHITE SOLID FABRIC:

- Cut 6 strips 2½" (6.5 cm) × WOF. Cut 12 strips 2½" × 9½" (6.5 × 24 cm) and 12 strips 2½" × 7½" (6.5 × 19 cm) from the strips.
- Cut 6 strips 5" (12.5 cm) × WOF. Cut 48 pieces A from the strips.

FROM CHARCOAL SOLID FABRIC:

- Cut 7 strips 5½" (14 cm) × WOF. Cut 48 pieces G from the strips.
- Cut 17 strips 2½" (6.5 cm) × WOF. Cut 17 strips 2½" × 21½" (6.5 × 54.5 cm) from the strips for sashing.
- From a 2½" (6.5 cm) strip remnant, cut 6 squares 2½" × 2½" (6.5 × 6.5 cm) for cornerstones.

FROM BACKING FABRIC:

- Cut 2 rectangles 98" (249 cm) × WOF.

FROM BINDING FABRIC:

- Cut 9 strips 2½" (6.5 cm) × WOF.

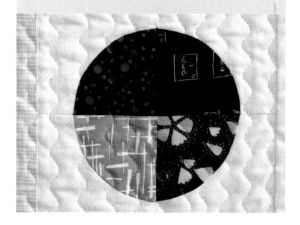

MAKING THE BLOCKS

Unfinished block size: 21½" × 21½" (53.5 × 53.5 cm) This quilt has twelve blocks.

1 Sew together the curved pieces A and B **(fig. 1)** as follows:

- Sew 12 gray print B pieces to 12 white A pieces.
- Sew 12 fuchsia print B pieces to 12 white A pieces.
- Sew 12 orange print B pieces to 12 white A pieces.
- Sew 12 blue print B pieces to 12 white A pieces.

Press the seams toward the B pieces. You will have a total of forty-eight small quarter-circle units. Trim the units to 4" × 4" (10 × 10 cm) square.

2 Sew each blue/white unit to each orange/white unit, matching adjacent seams. Press the seams open. Do the same with the fuchsia/white units and gray/white units **(fig. 2)**.

3 Sew the orange/blue units to the fuchsia/gray units, matching the adjacent seams to create the "tennis balls" **(fig. 2)**. Press the seams open, and trim the units to 7½" × 7½" (19 × 19 cm) square. Make a total of twelve tennis ball units.

4 With the "tennis ball" colors oriented as shown **(fig. 3)**, put together the Log Cabin style block as follows:

- Sew a 2½" × 7½" (6.5 × 19 cm) white strip to the right side of a tennis ball unit. Press the seam toward the white strip.
- Sew a 2½" × 9½" (6.5 × 24 cm) white strip to the top. Press the seam toward the white strip.
- Sew a 2½" × 9½" (6.5 × 24 cm) yellow stripe strip to the left side. Press the seam toward the yellow strip.
- Sew a 2½" × 11½" (6.5 × 29 cm) yellow stripe strip to the bottom. Press the seam toward the yellow strip.
- Sew a 2½" × 11½" (6.5 × 29 cm) yellow stripe strip to the right side. Press the seam toward the yellow strip.
- Sew a 2½" × 13½" (6.5 x 34.5 cm) yellow stripe strip to the top. Press the seam toward the yellow strip.

Repeat to make a total of twelve.

5 Sew a 4½" × 13½" (11.5 x 34.5 cm) green solid strip to top and bottom of each Log Cabin block **(fig. 4)**. Press the seams toward the green strips.

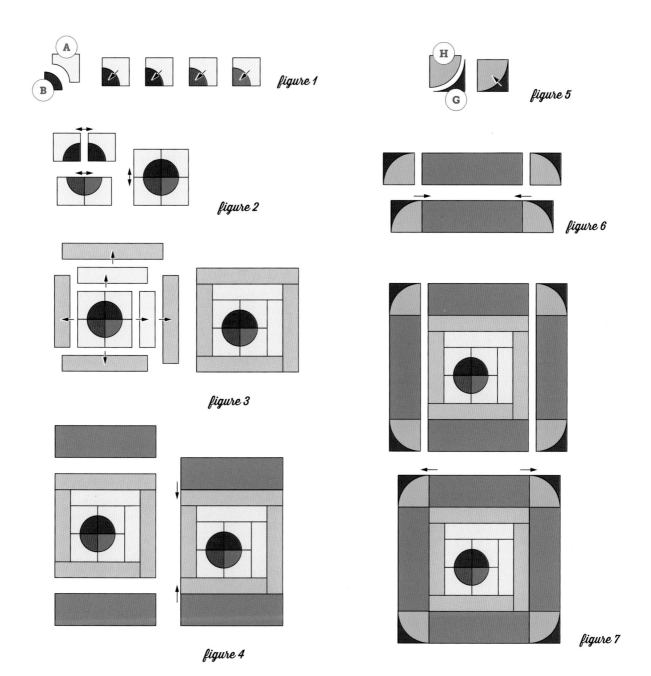

figure 1

figure 2

figure 3

figure 4

figure 5

figure 6

figure 7

6 Sew each charcoal solid piece G to each green print piece H **(fig. 5)**. Press the seams toward piece H. Trim the unit to 4½" × 4½" (11.5 × 11.5 cm), leaving a ¼" (6 mm) seam allowance on piece G.

7 Sew a green/charcoal unit to each end of the remaining twenty-four green solid strips 4½" × 13½" (11.5 × 34.5 cm) **(fig. 6).** Press the seams toward the green strips.

8 Sew these strips to the sides of each Log Cabin block, aligning adjacent seams, to complete twelve blocks **(fig. 7)**. Press the seams toward the green strip.

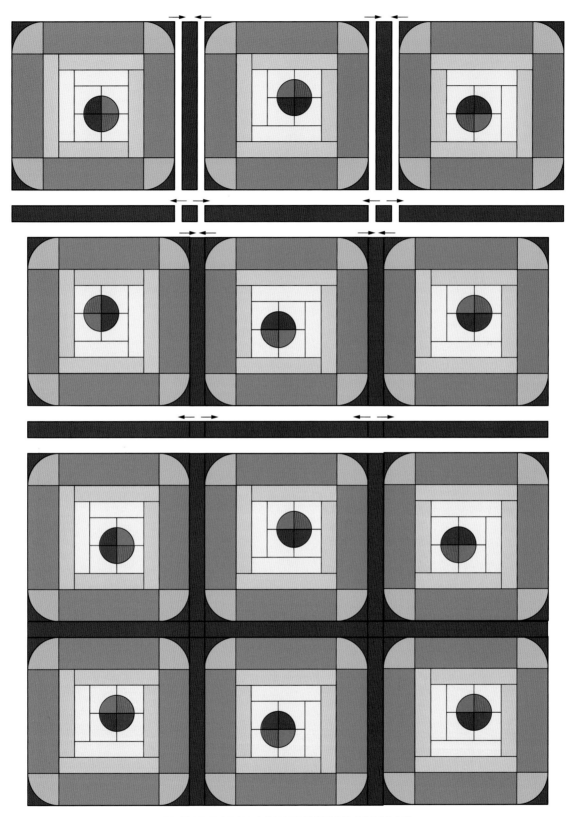

TENNIS MATCH CONSTRUCTION DIAGRAM

MAKING THE QUILT TOP

1 Arrange the blocks into four rows of three blocks each, as shown in the Tennis Match Construction Diagram, turning the blocks to create the "bouncing ball" effect. For each row, sew a charcoal sashing strip between the blocks. Press the seams toward the charcoal strip.

2 Sew the two charcoal cornerstone squares between three charcoal sashing strips to make three horizontal sashing rows.

3 Sew the block rows and sashings together to complete the quilt top, aligning all adjacent seams.

FINISHING

1 Refer to Finishing Your Quilt (page 132) or use your favorite methods to layer and baste the quilt top, batting, and backing.

2 Quilt as desired. I quilted wavy, vertical lines all across the quilt top.

3 Bind your quilt using my French double-fold binding method as described in Binding (page 139) or your own preferred method.

finished size
60" × 84" (152.5 × 213 cm)

designed and pieced by
ANGELA PINGEL

quilted by
KRISTA WITHERS

MATERIALS

Fabric amounts are based on yardage with a usable width of 42" (106.5 cm). Fat quarters are 18" × 22" (45.5 × 56 cm).

5⅛ yd (4.7 m) light blue print fabric

Note: Choose 1 medium and 1 dark value for each of the following fat quarters:

» 2 fat quarters orange print fabrics (orange #1 and #2)

» 2 fat quarters yellow print fabrics (yellow #1 and #2)

» 2 fat quarters purple print fabrics (purple #1 and #2)

» 2 fat quarters pink print fabrics (pink #1 and #2)

5¼ yd (4.8 m) backing fabric

⅝ yd (57 cm) binding fabric

68" × 92" (173 × 234 cm) batting

TOOLS

Template patterns M and N (small); Y and Z (medium); W and X (large)

Template plastic or paper

CUTTING

WOF = width of fabric

FROM LIGHT BLUE PRINT FABRIC:

• Cut 7 strips 12½" (31.5 cm) × WOF. Cut 20 squares 12½" × 12½" (31.5 × 31.5 cm) from the strips.

• Cut 5 strips 6½" (16.5 cm) × WOF. Cut 27 squares 6½" × 6½" (16.5 × 16.5 cm) from the strips.

• Cut 2 strips 6" (15 cm) × WOF. Cut 12 squares 6" × 6" (15 × 15 cm) from the strips. Cut 1 piece Y from each square.

• Cut 1 strip 3½" (9 cm) × WOF. Cut 11 squares 3½" × 3½" (9 × 9 cm) from the strip.

• Cut 1 strip 5½" (14 cm) × WOF. Cut 4 squares 5½" × 5½" (14 × 14 cm) from the strip.

continued on the next page >

the pattern

BUTTERFLIES
QUILT

the mix

A scattering of lively, curved butterfly motifs of all sizes, in charming prints

I'm probably not supposed to have favorites, but I can't help it. This is my favorite quilt in the book. It is the perfect balance of function and whimsy. The curves are so charming in this quilt. I used them sparingly for optimum impact. Because this quilt has a large amount of negative space, the blocks come together quickly. And, with its organic nature and movement, this is an extremely forgiving pattern. Drop everything you are doing and make this one! I promise it is a quilt that will make you smile the whole time you are creating it.

- Cut 4 strips 4½" (11.5 cm) × WOF. Cut 33 squares 4½" × 4½" (11.5 × 11.5 cm) from the strips. Cut 1 piece M from each square.
- Cut 2 strips 7½" (19 cm) × WOF. Cut 6 squares 7½" × 7½" (19 × 19 cm) from the strips. Cut 1 piece W from each square.
- Cut 3 strips 2½" (6.5 cm) × WOF. Cut 2 pieces 2½" × 12½" (6.5 × 31.5 cm) and 1 piece 2½" × 10½" (6.5 × 26.5 cm) from 2 strips. Cut 2 pieces 2½" × 10½" (6.5 × 26.5 cm) from remaining strip for a total of (4) 2½" × 12½" (6.5 × 31.5 cm) and (4) 2½" × 10½" (6.5 × 26.5 cm).

FROM ORANGE PRINT FAT QUARTER #1 (BUTTERFLY BODY):
- Cut 1 strip 5½" × 22" (14 × 56 cm). Cut 2 squares 5½" × 5½" (14 × 14 cm) from the strip. Cut 1 piece Z from each square.
- Cut 1 strip 3½" × 22" (9 × 56 cm). Cut 2 squares 3½" × 3½" (9 × 9 cm) from the strip. Cut 1 piece N from each square.

FROM ORANGE PRINT FAT QUARTER #2 (BUTTERFLY WINGS):
- Cut 2 strips 5½" × 22" (14 × 56 cm). Cut 4 squares 5½" × 5½" (14 × 14 cm) from the strips. Cut 1 piece Z from each square.
- Cut 1 strip 3½" × 22" (9 × 56 cm). Cut 4 squares 3½" × 3½" (9 × 9 cm) from the strip. Cut 1 piece N from each square.

FROM YELLOW PRINT FAT QUARTER #1 (BUTTERFLY BODY):
- Cut 1 strip 5½" × 22" (14 × 56 cm). Cut 2 squares 5½" × 5½" (14 × 14 cm) from the strip. Cut each square into 1 piece Z.
- Cut 1 strip 3½" × 22" (9 × 56 cm). Cut 2 squares 3½" × 3½" (9 × 9 cm) from the strip. Cut 1 piece N from each square.

FROM YELLOW PRINT FAT QUARTER #2 (BUTTERFLY WINGS):
- Cut 2 strips 5½" × 22" (14 × 56 cm). Cut 4 squares 5½" × 5½" (14 × 14 cm) from the strips. Cut 1 piece Z from each square.
- Cut 1 strip 3½" × 22" (9 × 56 cm). Cut 4 squares 3½" × 3½" (9 × 9 cm) from the strip. Cut 1 piece N from each square.

FROM PINK PRINT FAT QUARTER #1 (BUTTERFLY BODY):
- Cut 1 strip 3½" × 22" (9 × 56 cm). Cut 2 squares 3½" × 3½" (9 × 9 cm) from the strip. Cut 1 piece N from each square.
- Cut 1 strip 6½" × 22" (16.5 × 56 cm). Cut 1 square 6½" × 6½" (16.5 × 16.5 cm) from the strip. Cut 1 piece X from the square.

FROM PINK PRINT FAT QUARTER #2 (BUTTERFLY WINGS):
- Cut 1 strip 3½" × 22" (9 × 56 cm). Cut 4 squares 3½" × 3½" (9 × 9 cm) from the strip. Cut 1 piece N from each square.
- Cut 1 strip 6½" × 22" (16.5 × 56 cm). Cut 2 squares 6½" × 6½" (16.5 × 16.5 cm) from the strip. Cut 1 piece X from each strip.

FROM PURPLE PRINT FAT QUARTER #1 (BUTTERFLY BODY):
- Cut 1 strip 3½" × 22" (9 × 56 cm). Cut 5 squares 3½" × 3½" (9 × 9 cm) from the strip. Cut 1 piece N from each square.
- Cut 1 strip 6½" × 22" (16.5 × 56 cm). Cut 1 square 6½" × 6½" (16.5 × 16.5 cm) from the strip. Cut 1 piece X from the square.

FROM PURPLE PRINT FAT QUARTER #2 (BUTTERFLY WINGS):
- Cut 2 strips 3½" × 22" (9 × 56 cm). Cut 10 squares 3½" × 3½" (9 × 9 cm) from the strips. Cut 1 piece N from each square.
- Cut 1 strip 6½" × 22" (16.5 × 56 cm). Cut 2 squares 6½" × 6½" (16.5 × 16.5 cm) from the strip. Cut 1 piece X from each square.

FROM BACKING FABRIC:
- Cut 2 rectangles 92" (234 cm) × WOF.

FROM BINDING FABRIC:
- Cut 8 strips 2½" (6.5 cm) × WOF.

TIP

Are butterflies not your thing? You can easily accommodate the pattern to resemble other winged creatures. Try using a black fabric for the body and a red with black polka dot fabric for the wings to create a ladybug. Or use a yellow/black stripe fabric for the body and yellow fabric for the wings to create a bumblebee. Appliquéd antennae create a more literal look for the creatures as well.

MAKING THE BLOCKS

Unfinished block size: 12½" × 12½" (31.5 × 31.5 cm) You will make butterfly units in three sizes for the blocks—eleven small, four medium, and two large. The small and medium butterfly units will be combined with the blue background pieces in different ways to form the full blocks. Each large butterfly unit is a complete block unto itself. The remaining blocks in the quilt are unpieced blue squares.

BASIC BUTTERFLY UNITS

Use the same basic method to make all three sizes of butterfly units. Begin by making quarter-circle unit pairs, then combine them to make butterfly units.

1 Sew together curved pieces M and N for the small butterflies **(fig. 1)** as follows:

- Sew 2 blue print pieces M to 2 orange print #1 pieces N.

- Sew 4 blue print pieces M to 4 orange print #2 pieces N.

- Sew 2 blue print pieces M to 2 yellow print #1 pieces N.

- Sew 4 blue print pieces M to 4 yellow print #2 pieces N.

- Sew 2 blue print pieces M to 2 pink print #1 pieces N.

- Sew 4 blue print pieces M to 4 pink print #2 pieces N.

- Sew 5 blue print pieces M to 5 purple print #1 pieces N.

- Sew 10 blue print pieces M to 10 purple print #2 pieces N.

Press the seams toward piece N. Trim each unit to 3½" × 3½" (9 × 9 cm) with a ¼" (6 mm) seam allowance on piece M. You will have thirty-three small quarter-circle units.

2 Sew together curved pieces Y and Z for the medium butterflies as follows:

- Sew 2 blue print pieces Y to 2 yellow print #1 pieces Z.

- Sew 4 blue print pieces Y to 4 yellow print #2 pieces Z.

- Sew 2 blue print pieces Y to 2 orange print #1 pieces Z.

- Sew 4 blue print pieces Y to 4 orange print #2 pieces Z.

Press the seams toward piece Z. Trim each unit to 5½" × 5½" (14 × 14 cm) with a ¼" (6 mm) seam allowance on piece Y. You will have twelve medium quarter-circle units.

3 Sew together curved pieces W and X for the large butterfly as follows:

- Sew 1 blue print piece W to 1 pink print #1 piece X.

- Sew 2 blue print pieces W to 2 pink print #2 pieces X.

- Sew 1 blue print piece W to 1 purple print #1 piece X.

- Sew 2 blue print pieces W to 2 purple print #2 pieces X.

3½"

3½"

figure 1

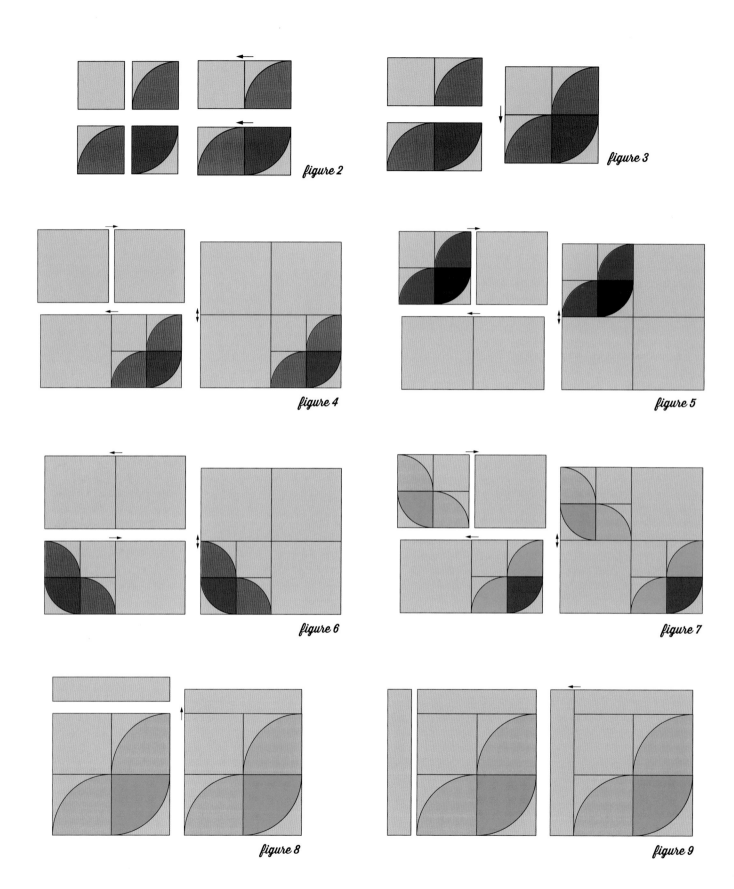

figure 2

figure 3

figure 4

figure 5

figure 6

figure 7

figure 8

figure 9

Press the seams toward piece X. Trim each unit to 6½" × 6½" (16.5 × 16.5 cm) with a ¼" (6 mm) seam allowance on piece W. You will have six large quarter-circle units.

4 Refer to **Figure 2** and **Figure 3** to assemble the small butterfly units. Sew a blue print square 3½" × 3½" (9 × 9 cm) to one wing unit. Press the seam toward the blue print square. Sew the remaining wing unit to the body unit. Press the seam toward the wing fabrics. Sew the two pieces together, matching the center seams. Press the seam open. Make a total of eleven small butterfly units.

5 Refer to **Figure 2** and **Figure 3** to assemble the medium butterfly units. Sew a blue print square 5½" × 5½" (14 × 14 cm) to one wing unit. Press the seam toward the blue print square. Sew the remaining wing unit to the body unit. Press the seam toward the wing fabrics. Sew the two pieces together, matching the center seams. Press the seam open. Make a total of four medium butterfly units.

6 Refer to **Figure 2** and **Figure 3** to assemble the large butterfly blocks. Sew a blue print square 6½" × 6½" (16.5 × 16.5 cm) to one wing unit. Press the seam toward the blue print square. Sew the remaining wing unit to the body unit. Press the seam toward the wing fabrics. Sew the two pieces together, matching the center seams. Press the seam open. Make a total of two large butterfly blocks.

SMALL BUTTERFLY BLOCKS

Refer to the Butterflies Construction Diagram (page 60) to correctly orient placement of the butterflies. There are four variations of the block made with small butterflies.

1 For Small Butterfly Block #1, make two blocks with purple print butterflies and one with an orange print butterfly. For each block, sew together two blue print squares 3½" × 3½" (9 × 9 cm). Press the seam to the right. Sew a blue print square 3½" × 3½" (9 × 9 cm) to an MN unit with fabric #1 in the bottom

right corner. Press the seam to the left. Sew together the top and bottom units, matching center seams **(fig. 4)**. Press the seam open.

2 For Small Butterfly Block #2, make three blocks with purple print butterflies. For each block, sew an MN unit with fabric #1 in the bottom right corner to a blue square 3½" × 3½" (9 × 9 cm). Press the seam to the right. Sew together two blue print squares 3½" × 3½" (9 × 9 cm). Press the seam to the left. Sew together the top and bottom units, matching center seams **(fig. 5)**. Press the seam open.

3 For Small Butterfly Block #3, make one block with an orange print butterfly. Sew together two blue print squares 3½" × 3½" (9 × 9 cm). Press the seam to the left. Sew an MN unit with fabric #1 in the bottom left corner to a blue print square 3½" × 3½" (9 × 9 cm). Press the seam to the right. Sew together the top and bottom units, matching center seams **(fig. 6)**. Press the seam open.

4 For Small Butterfly Block #4, make two blocks with one yellow print butterfly and one pink print butterfly. For each block, sew an MN unit with fabric #1 in the top left corner to a blue square 3½" × 3½" (9 × 9 cm). Press the seam to the right. Sew a blue print square 3½" × 3½" (9 × 9 cm) to an MN block with fabric #1 in the bottom right corner. Press the seam to the left. Sew together the top and bottom units, matching center seams **(fig. 7)**. Press the seam open.

MEDIUM BUTTERFLY BLOCKS

Make four blocks.

1 For each block, sew a blue print strip 2½" × 10½" (6.5 × 26.5 cm) to the top of a YZ block with fabric #1 in the bottom right corner **(fig. 8)**. Press the seam toward the strip.

2 Sew a blue print strip 2½" × 12½" (6.5 × 31.5 cm) to the left side **(fig. 9)**. Press the seam toward the strip. You will have two yellow print and two orange print blocks.

MAKING THE QUILT TOP

1 Refer to the Butterflies Construction Diagram to lay out seven rows of five blocks each. Use the small, medium, and large butterfly blocks along with the twenty blue squares 12½" × 12½" (31.5 × 31.5 cm). Note the block size, color, and orientation.

2 Sew the blocks into rows as shown. Press the seams in one direction, alternating for adjacent rows.

3 Sew the rows together to make the quilt top. Press seams in one direction.

FINISHING

1 Refer to Finishing Your Quilt (page 132) or use your favorite methods to layer and baste the quilt top, batting, and backing.

2 Quilt as desired. Longarm quilter Krista Withers shows off her talent with her creative quilting. She added swirling gusts of wind, straight-line sections, and detailed quilting on each butterfly.

3 Bind your quilt using my French double-fold binding method as described in Binding (page 139) or your own preferred method.

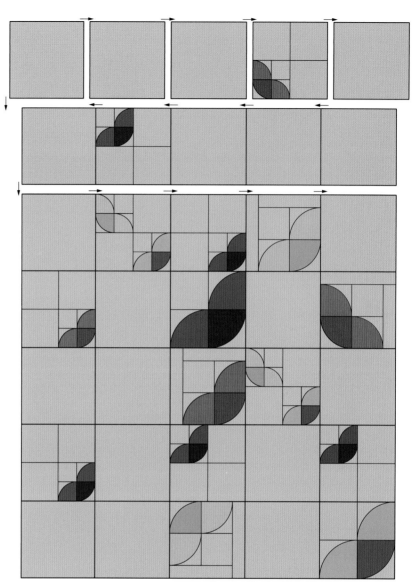

BUTTERFLIES CONSTRUCTION DIAGRAM

finished size
42" × 42" (106.5 × 106.5 cm)

designed, pieced, and quilted by
ANGELA PINGEL

MATERIALS

Fabric amounts are based on yardage with a usable width of 42" (106.5 cm), unless other-wise noted.

⅓ yd (30.5 cm) green print fabric

⅝ yd (57 cm) light blue print fabric

1 yd (91.5 cm) dark blue print fabric

1 yd (91.5 cm) yellow print fabric

⅝ yd (57 cm) orange print fabric

⅜ yd (34.5 cm) brown print fabric

1½ yd (137 cm) of 54" (137 cm) wide home decorator-weight backing fabric (or 2⅞ yd [2.7 m] of 45" [114.5 cm] wide fabric)

½ yd (45.5 cm) binding fabric

50" × 50" (127 × 127 cm) batting

TOOLS

Template patterns E and F or 7" (18 cm) AccuQuilt die and cutter (page 13)

Template plastic or paper (if using patterns)

CUTTING

WOF = width of fabric

FROM GREEN PRINT FABRIC:
• Cut 1 strip 9" (23 cm) × WOF. Cut 4 pieces F from the strips.

FROM LIGHT BLUE PRINT FABRIC:
• Cut 2 strips 10" (25.5 cm) × WOF. From these strips, cut 4 pieces E and 8 pieces F.

FROM DARK BLUE PRINT FABRIC:
• Cut 3 strips 10" (25.5 cm) × WOF. From these strips, cut 8 pieces E and 12 pieces F.

continued on the next page >

the pattern

MEDALLION
BABY
QUILT

the mix

The classic Love Ring design, splashed with rainbow ripples of bright prints

This colorful and cheerful quilt is perfect for the newest baby in your life. The pattern trans-lates well for either a boy or a girl, and the large blocks go together like a breeze. Consider mak-ing this quilt with a high-loft polyester batting and securely hand tying it to create a special, extra soft play mat for the baby. Think outside the box and try this with flannel or even cuddle fabrics for the ultimate snuggle factor.

FROM YELLOW PRINT FABRIC:
- Cut 3 strips 10" (25.5 cm) × WOF. From these strips, cut 12 pieces E and 8 pieces F.

FROM ORANGE PRINT FABRIC:
- Cut 2 strips 10" (25.5 cm) × WOF. From these strips cut 8 pieces E and 4 pieces F.

FROM BROWN PRINT FABRIC:
- Cut 1 strip 10" (25.5 cm) × WOF. Cut 4 pieces E from the strip.

FROM BACKING FABRIC:
- Cut 1 square 50" × 50" (127 × 127 cm) from home decorator fabric, or 2 rectangles 50" (127 cm) × WOF of 45" (114.5 cm) wide fabric.

FROM BINDING FABRIC:
- Cut 5 strips 2½" (6.5 cm) × WOF.

MAKING THE BLOCKS

Unfinished block size: 7½" × 7½" (19 × 19 cm). This quilt has thirty-six blocks.

1 Sew together all the pieces E and F as follows:

- Sew 4 green print pieces F to 4 light blue print pieces E.

- Sew 8 light blue print pieces F to 8 dark blue print pieces E.

- Sew 12 dark blue print pieces F to 12 yellow print pieces E.

- Sew 8 yellow print pieces F to 8 orange print pieces E.

- Sew 4 orange print pieces F to 4 brown print pieces E.

You will have a total of thirty-six quarter-circle blocks.

2 Press all seams toward the F piece. Trim the blocks to 7½" × 7½" (19 × 19 cm) square.

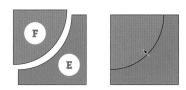

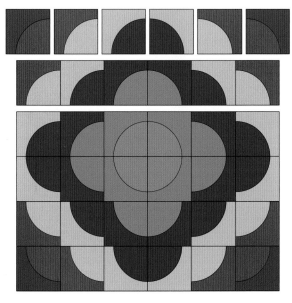

MEDALLION BABY CONSTRUCTION DIAGRAM

TIP

Home decorator-weight fabric is usually heavier and more durable than regular cotton, and it's wider so you don't have to piece the back. If you prefer, substitute any 45" (114.5 cm) wide cotton print.

MAKING THE QUILT TOP

1 Arrange the blocks into six rows of six blocks per row, as shown in the Medallion Baby Construction Diagram. Pay careful attention to the block orientation and color placement.

2 Sew the blocks together into rows, matching adjacent seams. Press the seams, alternating directions for each row.

3 Sew the rows together, matching adjacent seams. Press the seams in one direction.

FINISHING

1 Refer to Finishing Your Quilt (page 132) or use your favorite methods to layer and baste the quilt top, batting, and backing.

2 Quilt as desired. I echo quilted the center circle with concentric circles, then outlined each curve with channels filled with assorted free-motion stitches.

3 Bind your quilt using my French double-fold binding method as described in Binding (page 139) or your own preferred method.

finished size
56" × 72" (142 × 183 cm)

designed, pieced, and quilted by
ANGELA PINGEL

MATERIALS

Fabric amounts are based on yardage with a usable width of 42" (106.5 cm). Charm squares are 5" × 5" (12.5 × 12.5 cm).

$2^5/_8$ yd (2.4 m) white solid fabric

$^2/_3$ yd (61 cm) navy print fabric

144 assorted charm squares

$1^7/_8$ yd (1.7 m) orange print fabric for the borders

$3^5/_8$ yd (3.3 m) backing fabric

$^5/_8$ yd (57 cm) binding fabric

64" × 80" (162.5 × 203 cm) batting

TOOLS

Template patterns C and D or 4" (10 cm) Sizzix die and cutter (page 13)

Template plastic or paper (if using patterns)

CUTTING

WOF = width of fabric; LOF = length of fabric

FROM WHITE SOLID FABRIC:
• Cut 18 strips 5" (12.5 cm) × WOF. From these, cut the following:
  » From 8 strips, cut 96 pieces C.
  » From 10 strips, cut 96 pieces D.

FROM NAVY PRINT FABRIC:
• Cut 4 strips 5" (12.5 cm) × WOF. Cut 48 pieces C from the strips.

FROM CHARM SQUARES:
• Cut 48 pieces C.
• Cut 96 pieces D.

FROM ORANGE PRINT FABRIC:
• Cut a rectangle 64½" (164 cm) × WOF. Cut 2 strips 4½" (11.5 cm) × LOF and 2 strips 4½" × 64½" (11.5 × 164 cm).

FROM BACKING FABRIC:
• Cut 2 rectangles 64" (162.5 cm) × WOF.

FROM BINDING FABRIC:
• Cut 7 strips 2½" (6.5 cm) × WOF.

the pattern

ARABIAN NIGHTS QUILT

the mix

An enchanting "Persian carpet" of prints in a variety of scales shakes up the traditional Love Ring formula.

Arabian nights are calling, and the pull is strong. This traditional pattern is spiced up with 144 unique charm squares. With twelve large, tiled blocks, this is a perfect choice for a quilting bee. I pieced this quilt from Anna Maria Horner fabrics, as an homage to the beauty and cohesiveness of her many different fabric lines. Using a die-cutter helped make quick work of cutting the many pieces for this quilt.

figure 1

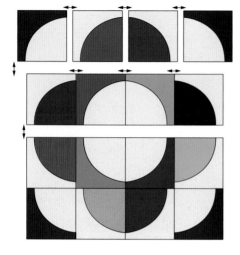

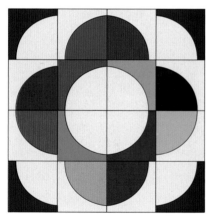

figure 2

MAKING THE BLOCKS

Unfinished block size: 16½" × 16½" (42 × 42 cm)
This quilt has twelve large, tiled blocks, each composed of sixteen small blocks.

1 Sew together all the pieces C and D as follows **(fig. 1)**:

- Sew 48 navy print pieces C to 48 white solid pieces D. Press the seams toward piece C.

- Sew 48 charm square pieces C to 48 white solid pieces D. Press the seams toward piece C.

- Sew 96 white solid pieces C to 96 charm square pieces D. Press the seams toward piece C.

You will have a total of 192 quarter-circle units 4½" × 4½" (11.5 × 11.5 cm).

2 Assemble the twelve large, tiled blocks using the units from Step 1. Each block is made up of sixteen small units: four navy/white units, four charm/white units, and eight white/charm units. Orient the pieces as shown in **Figure 2**, and sew the blocks together. Press all seams open.

MAKING THE QUILT TOP

1 Refer to the Arabian Nights Construction Diagram to lay out the quilt top center in four rows of three large tiled blocks each. Sew together each row, aligning adjacent seams; press all seams open. Sew together the four rows to complete the quilt top center. Press all seams in one direction.

2 Sew the orange print borders to the quilt. Sew a strip 4½" × 64½" (11.5 × 164 cm) to each side of the quilt. Press the seams toward the border. Sew a strip 4½" × 64½" (11.5 × 164 cm) to the quilt top and bottom. Press the seams toward the border.

TIP

When assembling your blocks, try alternating warm and cool colors for a thoroughly balanced look to your quilt.

ARABIAN NIGHTS CONSTRUCTION DIAGRAM

FINISHING

1   Refer to Finishing Your Quilt (page 132) or use your favorite methods to layer and baste the quilt top, batting, and backing.

2   Quilt as desired. I quilted a simple crosshatch pattern over the whole quilt top.

3   Bind your quilt using my French double-fold binding method as described in Binding (page 139) or your own preferred method.

TIP

Don't have enough charms? Look online for charm swaps, or start one of your own! That's how I accumulated all of my charms for this quilt.

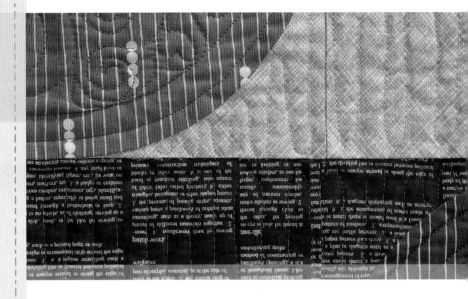

MATERIALS

Fabric amounts are based on yardage with a usable width of 42" (106.5 cm).

1½ yd (137 cm) blue print fabric

2¼ yd (2 m) orange print fabric

2¾ yd (2.5 m) dark gray text print fabric

2⅛ yd (1.9 m) light gray print fabric

6⅛ yd (5.6 m) backing fabric

¾ yd (68.5 cm) binding fabric

81" × 98" (206 × 250 cm) batting

TOOLS

Template patterns Y and Z

Template plastic or paper

CUTTING

WOF = width of fabric

FROM BLUE PRINT FABRIC:

- Cut 1 piece 50½" (128.5 cm) × WOF. Refer to Blue Print Cutting Diagram (page 75) to cut the following from this piece:
  - » Cut 1 strip 2½" × 50½" (6.5 × 128.5 cm).
  - » Cut 2 squares 10½" × 10½" (26.5 × 26.5 cm).
  - » Cut 1 rectangle 5½" × 10½" (14 × 26.5 cm).
  - » Cut 3 strips 2½" × 20½" (6.5 × 52 cm).
  - » Cut 1 strip 2½" × 15½" (6.5 × 39.5 cm).
  - » Cut 12 squares 5½" × 5½" (14 × 14 cm). Cut 1 piece Z from each square.

FROM ORANGE PRINT FABRIC:

- Cut 2 strips 5½" (14 cm) × WOF. Cut 7 squares 5½" × 5½" (14 × 14 cm) from one strip and 1 square 5½" × 5½" (14 × 14 cm) from the second strip for a total of 8 pieces. Cut 1 piece Z from each square.

continued on the next page >

TELEPORT QUILT

the mix

Straight shots of strips with a few random, curved ovals for punch

The perfect quilt for your favorite sci-fi fan, Teleport invokes images of movement and mathematical binary systems. I styled the fabrics deliberately to show the quilt in a masculine light. We all know how hard it is to find a pattern for the men in our lives, especially those who might not love quilts as much as we do (gasp!). But don't feel limited by the palette. With a basic four-color fabric scheme, it's easy to change the feel with just a few simple alternative fabrics.

finished size
73" × 90" (185 × 229 cm)

designed, pieced, and quilted by
ANGELA PINGEL

- Cut 2 strips 6½" (16.5 cm) × WOF. Cut 6 squares 6½" × 6½" (16.5 × 16.5 cm) from one strip and 2 squares 6½" × 6½" (16.5 × 16.5 cm) from the second strip for a total of 8 pieces. Cut 1 piece Y from each square.
- Cut 1 piece 51½" (131 cm) × WOF. Refer to Orange Print Cutting Diagram (page 75) to cut the following from this piece:
  » Cut 1 strip 4½" × 50½" (11.5 × 128.5 cm).
  » Cut 1 strip 4½" × 20½" (11.5 × 52 cm).
  » Cut 2 strips 3½" × 45½" (9 × 115.5 cm).
  » Cut 1 strip 4½" × 40½" (11.5 × 103 cm).
  » Cut 2 strips 5½" × 20½" (14 × 52 cm).
  » Cut 4 strips 5½" × 15½" (14 × 39.5 cm).
  » Cut 4 rectangles 5½" × 10½" (14 × 26.5 cm).

FROM DARK GRAY TEXT PRINT FABRIC:
- Cut 3 strips 6½" (16.5 cm) × WOF. Cut 16 squares 6½" × 6½" (16.5 × 16.5 cm) from the strips. Cut 1 piece Y from each square.
- Cut 1 strip 5½" (14 cm) × WOF. Cut 4 squares 5½" × 5½" (14 × 14 cm) from the strip. Cut 1 piece Z from each square.
- Cut 1 piece 50½" (128.5 cm) × WOF. Refer to Dark Gray Text Print Cutting Diagram 1 (page 75) to cut the following from this piece:
  » Cut 1 strip 8½" × 50½" (21.5 × 128.5 cm).
  » Cut 2 strips 4½" × 50½" (11.5 × 128.5 cm).
  » Cut 1 strip 8½" × 40½" (21.5 × 103 cm).
  » Cut 3 rectangles 5½" × 10½" (14 × 26.5 cm).
  » Cut 2 strips 4½" × 15½" (11.5 × 39.5 cm).

- Cut 1 piece 20½" (52 cm) × WOF. Refer to Dark Gray Text Print Cutting Diagram 2 (page 75) to cut the following from this piece:
  » Cut 6 strips 4½" × 20½" (11.5 × 52 cm).
  » Cut 1 strip 8½" × 20½" (21.5 × 52 cm).

FROM LIGHT GRAY PRINT FABRIC:
- Cut 1 piece 50½" (128.5 cm) × WOF. Refer to Light Gray Print Cutting Diagram 1 (page 76) to cut the following from this piece:
  » Cut 1 strip 8½" × 50½" (21.5 × 128.5 cm).
  » Cut 1 strip 8½" × 40½" (21.5 × 103 cm).
  » Cut 4 strips 5½" × 45½" (14 × 115.5 cm).
- Cut 1 piece 20½" (52 cm) × WOF. Refer to Light Gray Print Cutting Diagram 2 (page 76) to cut the following from this piece:
  » Cut 1 strip 8½" × 20½" (21.5 × 52 cm).
  » Cut 3 rectangles 5½" × 10½" (14 × 26.5 cm).
  » Cut 4 squares 5½" × 5½" (14 × 14 cm). Cut 1 piece Z from each square.
  » Cut 4 squares 6" × 6" (15 × 15 cm). Cut 1 piece Y from each square.

FROM BACKING FABRIC:
- Cut 3 pieces 73" (185 cm) × WOF.

FROM BINDING FABRIC:
- Cut 9 strips 2½" (6.5 cm) × WOF.

TIP

When you are cutting the pieces, pay careful attention to the orientation of directional fabrics such as the text print. Directional fabrics are very effective in this quilt design, but it is easy to place them in the wrong direction. A design wall is very helpful for laying out the pieces for this quilt.

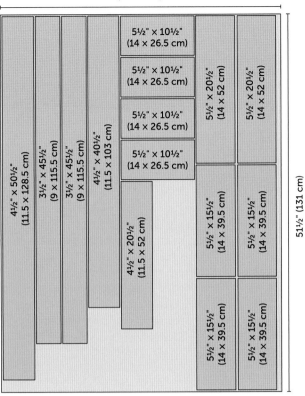

ORANGE PRINT CUTTING DIAGRAM

BLUE PRINT CUTTING DIAGRAM

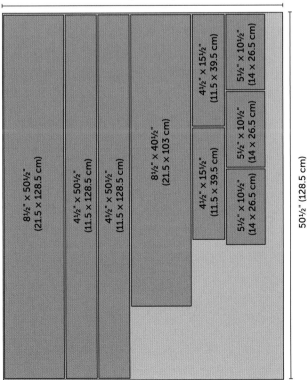

DARK GRAY TEXT PRINT CUTTING DIAGRAM 1

DARK GRAY TEXT PRINT CUTTING DIAGRAM 2

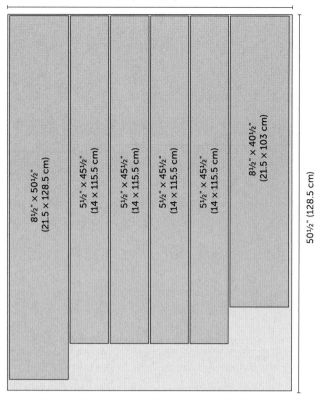

LIGHT GRAY PRINT CUTTING DIAGRAM 1

42" (106.5 cm)

8½" × 50½" (21.5 × 128.5 cm)

5½" × 45½" (14 × 115.5 cm)

5½" × 45½" (14 × 115.5 cm)

5½" × 45½" (14 × 115.5 cm)

5½" × 45½" (14 × 115.5 cm)

8½" × 40½" (21.5 × 103 cm)

50½" (128.5 cm)

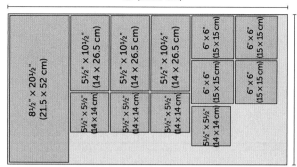

LIGHT GRAY PRINT CUTTING DIAGRAM 2

42" (106.5 cm)

8½" × 20½" (21.5 × 52 cm)

5½" × 10½" (14 × 26.5 cm)

5½" × 10½" (14 × 26.5 cm)

5½" × 10½" (14 × 26.5 cm)

6" × 6" (15 × 15 cm)

6" × 6" (15 × 15 cm)

5½" × 5½" (14 × 14 cm)

5½" × 5½" (14 × 14 cm)

5½" × 5½" (14 × 14 cm)

6" × 6" (15 × 15 cm)

6" × 6" (15 × 15 cm)

5½" × 5½" (14 × 14 cm)

20½" (52 cm)

MAKING THE QUILT TOP

This quilt is assembled in seven columns, which are then sewn together to complete the quilt top. You will complete the columns out of sequence, working first with columns 1 and 3, which contain orange curved pieces, and then with columns 2 and 6, which contain blue curved pieces. Columns 4, 5, and 7 are simply strips of one color.

QUARTER-CIRCLE UNITS

Begin by sewing together the curved pieces for all the columns.

1 Sew together curved pieces Y and Z **(fig. 1)** as follows:

- Sew 4 pieces Y in dark gray text print to 4 pieces Z in orange print.

- Sew 12 pieces Y in dark gray text print to 12 pieces Z in blue print.

- Sew 4 pieces Y in light gray print to 4 pieces Z in orange print.

- Sew 4 pieces Y in orange print to 4 pieces Z in dark gray text print.

- Sew 4 pieces Y in orange print to 4 pieces Z in light gray print.

Press the seams toward Z. You will have a total of twenty-eight quarter-circle units.

2 Trim units to 5½" × 5½" (14 × 14 cm), leaving a ¼" (6 mm) seam allowance on piece Y.

Z

Y

5½"

5½"

figure 1

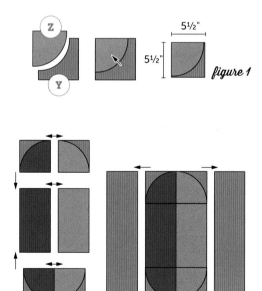

figure 2

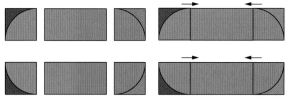

figure 3

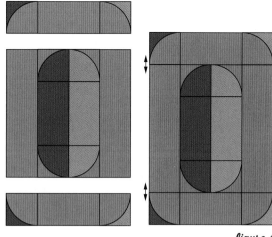

figure 4

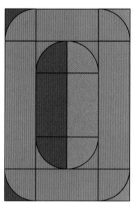

column 1

COLUMN 1

1 Refer to **Figure 2** to sew an orange Y/dark gray Z unit to an orange Y/light gray Z unit. Repeat to sew together a second pair. Make sure all the colors and curves are oriented as shown. Sew a dark gray rectangle 5½" × 10½" (14 × 26.5 cm) to a light gray rectangle 5½" × 10½" (14 × 26.5 cm) along the long sides. Press the seams open.

2 Refer to **Figure 2** to sew together the three units from Step 1, aligning adjacent seams. Press the seams toward the middle strips. Sew an orange print strip 5½" × 20½" (14 × 52 cm) to each side of the unit. Press the seams toward the orange print strips.

3 Refer to **Figure 3** to sew a dark gray Y/orange Z unit to the left end of an orange rectangle 5½" × 10½" (14 × 26.5 cm). Sew a light gray Y/orange Z unit to the other end of the rectangle. Make sure all the colors and curves are oriented as shown. Press the seams toward the orange rectangles.

4 Sew the units from Step 3 to the top and bottom of the unit constructed in steps 1 and 2, making sure to orient them as shown in **Figure 4**. Press the seams open.

5 Sew a dark gray strip 8½" × 20½" (21.5 × 52 cm) to the left edge of an orange strip 4½" × 20½" (11.5 × 52 cm). Sew a light gray strip 8½" × 20½" (21.5 × 52 cm) to the right edge. Repeat with a dark gray strip 8½" × 40½" (21.5 × 103 cm), an orange strip

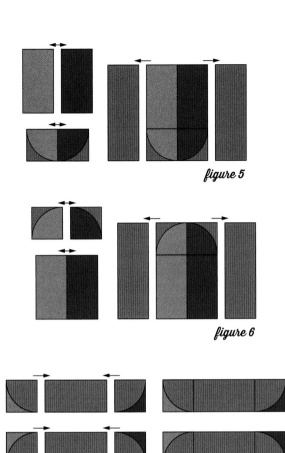

figure 5

figure 6

figure 7

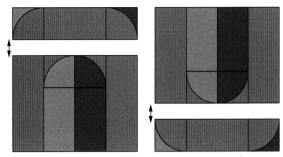

figure 8

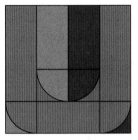

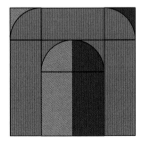

column 3

4½" × 40½" (11.5 × 103 cm), and a light gray strip 8½" × 40½" (21.5 × 103 cm). Press the seams toward the orange strips.

6 Sew together the three pieces created in the previous steps. Refer to the **Column 1** diagram to align the pieces with all the dark gray text prints on the left. The shorter strips are on the top, the rounded piece in the middle, and the longer strips at the bottom. This completes Column 1.

COLUMN 3

1 Refer to **Figure 5** to sew an orange Y/light gray Z unit to an orange Y/dark gray Z unit. Make sure all the colors and curves are oriented as shown. Sew a light gray rectangle 5½" × 10½" (14 × 26.5 cm) to a dark gray rectangle 5½" × 10½" (14 × 26.5 cm) along the long sides. Press the seams open. Sew together the pieces, with the light gray print on the left side and the strips at the top of the curved units. Press the seams open. Sew an orange strip 5½" × 15½" (14 × 39.5 cm) to each side; press toward the orange strips.

2 Refer to **Figure 6** to sew an orange Y/light gray Z unit to an orange Y/dark gray Z unit. Make sure all the colors and curves are oriented as shown. Sew a light gray rectangle 5½" × 10½" (14 × 26.5 cm) to a dark gray rectangle 5½" × 10½" (14 × 26.5 cm) along the long sides. Press the seams open. Sew together the pieces, with the light gray print on the left side and the strips at the bottom of the curved units. Align adjacent seams. Sew an orange strip 5½" × 15½" (14 × 39.5 cm) to each side of both units; press the seams toward the orange strips.

3 Refer to **Figure 7** to sew a light gray Y/orange Z unit to the left end of an orange rectangle 5½" × 10½" (14 × 26.5 cm). Sew a dark gray Y/orange Z unit to the other end of the rectangle. Make sure all the colors and curves are oriented as shown. Repeat with another identical three pieces, but orient the curves in the opposite direction as shown. Press the seams toward the orange strips.

4 Sew together the units as shown in **Figure 8**. Make sure all the colors and curves are oriented as shown. Press the seams open.

5 Sew a light gray strip 8½" × 50½" (21.5 × 128.5 cm) to the long left edge of an orange strip 4½" × 50½" (11.5 × 128.5 cm). Sew a dark gray strip 8½" × 50½" (21.5 × 128.5 cm) to the right edge. Press the seams toward orange strip.

6 Sew together the three pieces created in the previous steps. Align the pieces with all the light gray prints on the left as shown in the **Column 1** diagram. This completes Column 3.

COLUMN 2

1 Sew together two pairs of dark gray Y/blue Z units, oriented as shown **(fig. 9)**. Press the seams open.

2 Sew one unit from Step 1 to the top of a blue square 10½" × 10½" (26.5 × 26.5 cm), and one unit to the bottom. Press the seams toward the blue square.

3 Refer to the **Column 2** diagram to sew a dark gray strip 4½" × 50½" (11.5 × 128.5 cm) to each side of a blue strip 2½" × 50½" (6.5 × 128.5 cm). Sew a dark

gray strip 4½" × 20½" (11.5 × 52 cm) to each side of a blue strip 2½" × 20½" (6.5 × 52 cm). Press the seams toward the blue strip.

4 Sew together the three pieces from steps 2 and 3 as shown in the **Column 2** diagram. This completes Column 2.

figure 9

column 2

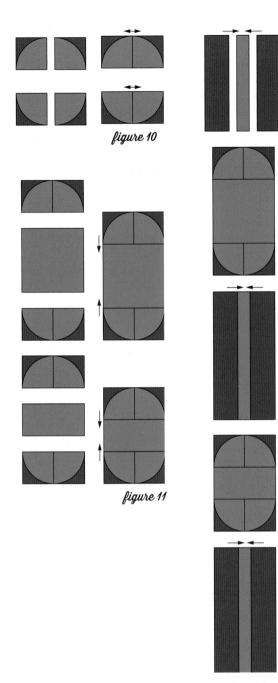

figure 10

figure 11

column 6

COLUMN 6

1 Sew together two pairs of dark gray Y/blue Z units oriented as shown **(fig. 10)**. Press the seams open. Sew a second set of each. Press the seams open.

2 Sew one set from Step 1 to the top and bottom of a blue rectangle 5½" × 10½" (14 × 26.5 cm) oriented as shown **(fig. 11)**. Press the seams toward the blue rectangle. Sew another set from Step 1 to the top and bottom of a blue square 10½" × 10½" (26.5 × 26.5 cm), oriented as shown. Press the seams toward the blue square.

3 Refer to the Column 6 diagram to sew a dark gray strip 4½" × 20½" (11.5 × 52 cm) to each long side of a blue strip 2½" × 20½" (6.5 × 52 cm). Sew a second identical set. Sew a dark gray strip 4½" × 15½" (11.5 × 39.5 cm) to each long side of a blue strip 2½" × 15½" (6.5 × 39.5 cm). Press seams toward blue strip.

4 Sew together the five pieces from steps 2 and 3. Place the short striped piece on top, then the long rounded piece, then a long striped piece, then the short rounded piece, and a long striped piece at the bottom as shown in the Column 6 diagram. This completes Column 6.

COLUMNS 4, 5, AND 7

1 Sew together two light gray strips 5½" × 45½" (14 × 115.5 cm) end to end to make Column 4. Press the seam open.

2 Sew together two orange strips 3½" × 45½" (9 × 115.5 cm) end to end to make Column 5. Press the seam open.

3 Sew together two light gray strips 5½" × 45½" (14 × 115.5 cm) end to end to make Column 7. Press the seam open.

column   1   2   3   4   5   6   7

TELEPORT CONSTRUCTION DIAGRAM

ASSEMBLY AND FINISHING

1   Refer to the Teleport Construction Diagram (page 81) to lay out the seven columns for the quilt top. Sew them together along the long sides. Press.

2   Refer to Finishing Your Quilt (page 132) or use your favorite methods to layer and baste the quilt top, batting, and backing.

3   Quilt as desired. I quilted a combination of long, dense loops back and forth, and echo quilted, filling in with free-motion swirls.

4   Bind your quilt using my French double-fold binding method as described in Binding (page 139) or your own preferred method.

TIP

Looking for alternate color schemes? Try switching out the orange and blue with dark and light shades of lime green for a computer tech look à la The Matrix. Or go for a '60s funky lava lamp look with bright shades of pink, purple, orange, and yellow.

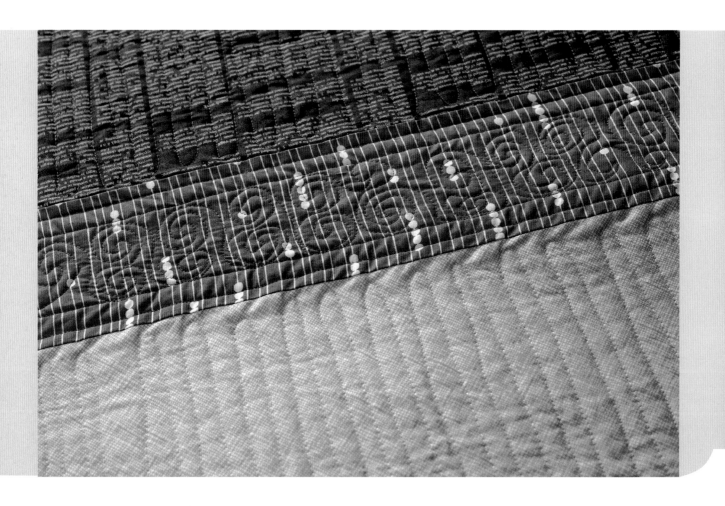

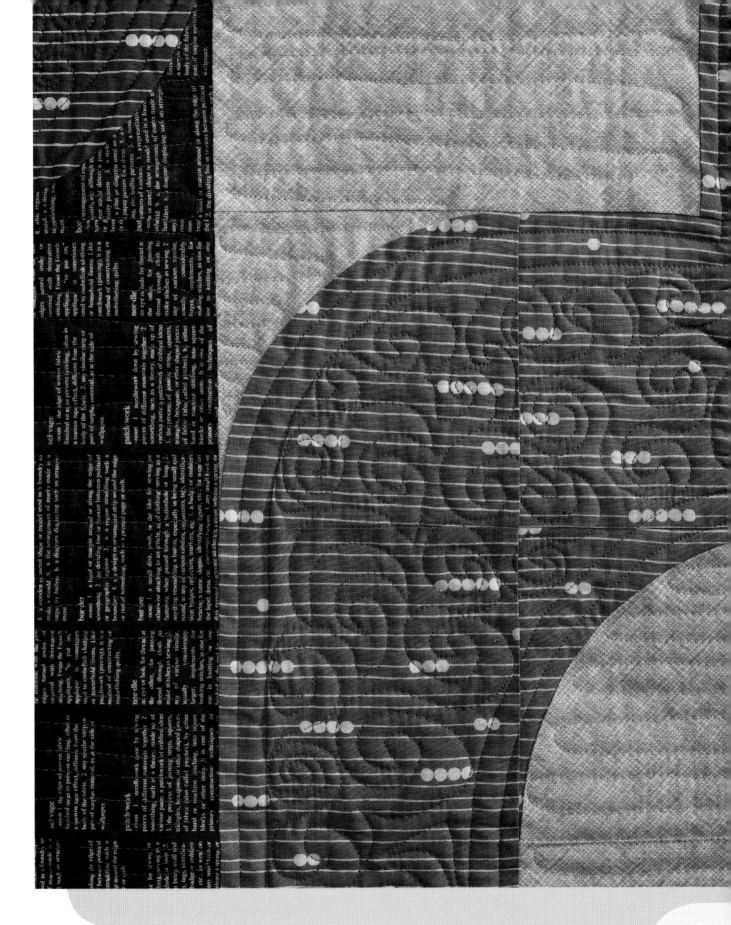

finished size
48" × 60" (122 × 152.5 cm)

designed, pieced, and quilted by
ANGELA PINGEL

MATERIALS

Fabric amounts are based on yardage with a usable width of 42" (106.5 cm). Fat quarters are 18" × 22" (45.5 × 56 cm).

4 fat quarters assorted blue print fabrics

4 fat quarters assorted mint print fabrics

4 fat quarters assorted fuchsia print fabrics

4 fat quarters assorted gold print fabrics

³⁄₈ yd (34.5 cm) focal fabric for Nine Patch block centers*

8 assorted ¼ yd (23 cm) neutral print fabrics for template pieces

4 assorted ¼ yd (23 cm) neutral print fabrics for Nine Patch blocks

4 fat quarters assorted neutral print fabrics for Nine Patch blocks

3¹⁄₃ yd (3 m) backing fabric

½ yd (45.5 cm) binding fabric

56" × 68" (142 × 173 cm) batting

*I chose a print that combines the colors of the other fabrics in the quilt.

TOOLS

Template patterns K and L

Template plastic or paper

CUTTING

WOF = width of fabric

FROM BLUE PRINT FABRICS:

• From 2 of the fabrics, cut 2 strips 4½" × 18" (11.5 × 45.5 cm) for a total of 4 strips. From the strips, cut 10 squares 4½" × 4½" (11.5 × 11.5 cm). Cut 1 piece L from each square.

• From the remaining 2 fabrics, cut 2 strips 4½" × 18" (11.5 × 45.5 cm) for a total of 4 strips.

continued on the next page >

the pattern

NINE PATCH
CURVES
QUILT

the mix

The perfect blend of two very traditional blocks, the Drunkard's Path and the Nine Patch

Chances are, if you have made even one traditionally styled quilt, then you've used one of these two block designs. Here the Nine Patch and Drunkard's Path blocks are married together in a truly seamless design. In this beautifully scrappy quilt, the possibilities for color schemes are endless.

FROM MINT PRINT FABRICS:

- From 2 of the fabrics, cut 2 strips 4½" × 18" (11.5 × 45.5 cm) for a total of 4 strips. From the strips, cut 10 squares 4½" × 4½" (11.5 × 11.5 cm). Cut 1 piece L from each square.
- From the remaining 2 fabrics, cut 2 strips 4½" × 18" (11.5 × 45.5 cm) for a total of 4 strips.

FROM FUCHSIA PRINT FABRICS:

- From 2 of the fabrics, cut 2 strips 4½" × 18" (11.5 × 45.5 cm) for a total of 4 strips. From the strips, cut 10 squares 4½" × 4½" (11.5 × 11.5 cm). Cut 1 piece L from each square.
- From the remaining 2 fabrics, cut 2 strips 4½" × 18" (11.5 × 45.5 cm) for a total of 4 strips.

FROM GOLD PRINT FABRICS:

- From 2 of the fabrics, cut 2 strips 4½" × 18" (11.5 × 45.5 cm) for a total of 4 strips. From the strips, cut 10 squares 4½" × 4½" (11.5 × 11.5 cm). Cut 1 piece L from each square.
- From the remaining 2 fabrics, cut 2 strips 4½" × 18" (11.5 × 45.5 cm) for a total of 4 strips.

FROM FOCAL FABRIC FOR NINE PATCH BLOCK CENTERS:

- Cut 2 strips 4½" (11.5 cm) × WOF.

FROM TEMPLATE NEUTRAL PRINT FABRICS:

- From 8 pieces ¼ yard (23 cm), cut 1 strip 6½" (16.5 cm) × WOF for a total of 8 strips. Cut 5 squares 6½" × 6½" (16.5 × 16.5 cm) from each strip. Cut 1 piece K from each square.

FROM NINE-PATCH NEUTRAL FABRICS:

- From 4 fat quarter pieces, cut 2 strips 4½" × 18" (11.5 × 45.5 cm) for a total of 8 strips.
- From 4 pieces ¼ yard (23 cm), cut 1 strip 4½" (11.5 cm) × WOF for a total of 4 strips.

FROM BACKING FABRIC:

- Cut 2 pieces 1⅔ yd (1.5 m) × WOF.

FROM BINDING FABRIC:

- Cut 6 strips 2½" (6.5 cm) × WOF.

MAKING THE BLOCKS

Unfinished block size: 12½" × 12½" (31.5 × 31.5 cm)
This quilt has ten Nine Patch blocks and ten Drunkard's Path curved blocks.

DRUNKARD'S PATH CURVED BLOCKS

1 Sew together the curved pieces K and L **(fig. 1)** as follows:

- Sew 10 blue print pieces L to 10 neutral print pieces K.
- Sew 10 fuchsia print pieces L to 10 neutral print pieces K.
- Sew 10 mint print pieces L to 10 neutral print pieces K.
- Sew 10 gold print pieces L to 10 neutral print pieces K.

Press the seams toward the L pieces. Trim the blocks to 6½" × 6½" (16.5 × 16.5 cm). You will have a total of forty quarter-circle units.

2 Sew each gold/neutral unit to each mint/neutral unit, matching the neutral sides. Press the seams open. Sew each blue/neutral unit to each fuchsia/neutral unit, matching the neutral sides **(fig. 2)**. Press the seams open.

3 Sew the gold/mint units to the blue/fuchsia units, matching the neutral fabrics and the center seams. Press the seams open. Fuchsia and yellow should be kitty-corner, and blue and mint should be kitty-corner. Repeat to make a total of ten Drunkard's Path blocks.

NINE PATCH BLOCKS

1 Sew a neutral fabric strip 4½" (11.5 cm) × WOF to either side of a focal strip 4½" × WOF **(fig. 3)**. Press the seams toward the focal strip. Repeat to create a second strip set.

2 Cross-cut each pieced strip set into five strips 4½" × 12½" (11.5 × 31.5 cm) for a total of ten pieces **(fig. 4)**.

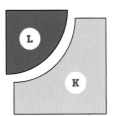

figure 1

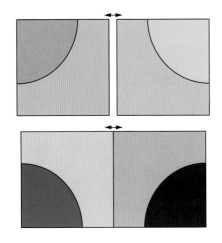
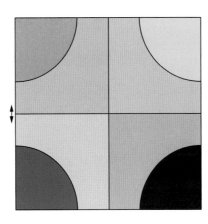

figure 2

TIP

Make this quilt more scrappy or less scrappy in a snap. All assorted neutral fabrics can be one fabric, or they can all be different scraps. The choice is yours!

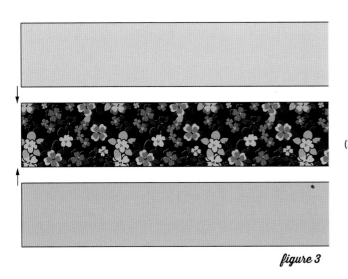

figure 3

4½" (11.5 cm)

12½" (31.5 cm)

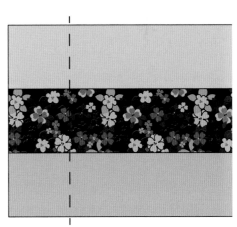

figure 4

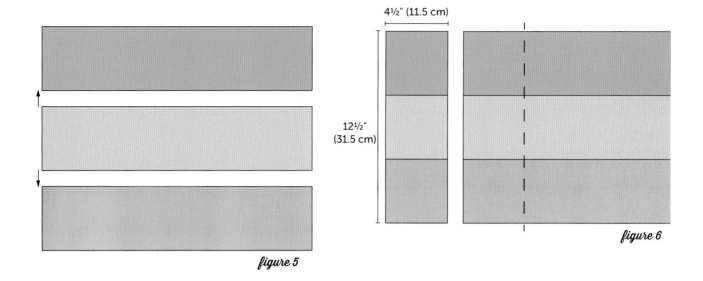

4½" (11.5 cm)

12½"
(31.5 cm)

figure 5

figure 6

TIP

Because this quilt is based on two blocks, the size is limited only by the number of blocks you want to make. You can easily make this quilt larger by adding extra rows and columns. It's the perfect way to use your scraps!

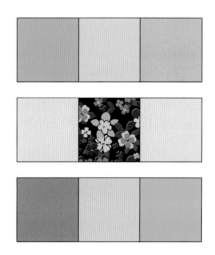

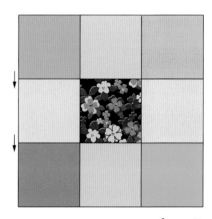

figure 7

3 Sew a colored strip 4½" × 18" (11.5 × 45.5 cm) to each side of a neutral print strip 4½" × 18" (11.5 × 45.5 cm) **(fig. 5)** as follows:

- Sew 2 strips with mint and gold.
- Sew 2 strips with blue and gold.
- Sew 2 strips with blue and fuchsia.
- Sew 2 strips with mint and fuchsia.

Press the seams toward the colored strips.

4 Cross-cut the pieced strip set from Step 3 into strips 4½" × 12½" (11.5 × 31.5 cm) **(fig. 6)** as follows:

- Cut 6 strips with mint and gold.
- Cut 4 strips with blue and gold.
- Cut 6 strips with blue and fuchsia.
- Cut 4 strips with mint and fuchsia.

NINE PATCH CONSTRUCTION DIAGRAM

- -

5 Assemble the Nine Patch block in three rows of strips 4½" × 12½" (11.5 × 31.5 cm). The middle row is always a neutral/focal/neutral strip. The top and bottom rows always match in groups of two colors, but the colors alternate left to right **(fig. 7)**. Assemble as follows:

- Sew 3 blocks with mint and gold.

- Sew 2 blocks with blue and gold.

- Sew 3 blocks with blue and fuchsia.

- Sew 2 blocks with mint and fuchsia.

Press the seams in one direction. You will have a total of ten Nine Patch blocks.

MAKING THE QUILT TOP

1 Arrange the blocks into five rows of four alternating blocks each, as shown in the Nine Patch Curves Construction Diagram (page 89). Rotate the blocks as necessary for color placement. Sew together the two Nine Patch blocks and two Drunkard's Path blocks in each row. Press the seams toward the Nine Patch blocks. Construct rows 1 through 5.

2 Sew the rows together to make the quilt top. Press the seams in one direction.

FINISHING

1 Refer to Finishing Your Quilt (page 132) or use your favorite methods to layer and baste the quilt top, batting, and backing.

2 Quilt as desired. I quilted an allover swirling pattern that adds movement to the quilt top.

3 Bind your quilt using my French double-fold binding method as described in Binding (page 139) or your own preferred method.

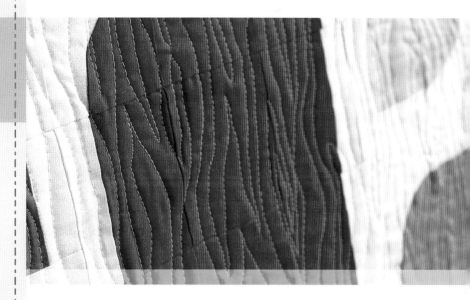

finished size
31½" × 31½" (80 × 80 cm)

designed, pieced, and quilted by
ANGELA PINGEL

MATERIALS

Fabric amounts are based on yardage with a usable width of 42" (106.5 cm). Fat quarters are 18" × 22" (45.5 × 56 cm).

¾ yd (68.5 cm) white solid fabric

½ yd (45.5 cm) blue solid fabric

1 fat quarter orange solid fabric

1 fat quarter red solid fabric

1 fat quarter lime green solid fabric

1 fat quarter purple solid fabric

1⅛ yd (102 cm) backing fabric

⅜ yd (34.5 cm) binding fabric

39" × 39" (99 × 99 cm) batting

TOOLS

Template patterns A and B or 3½" (9 cm) AccuQuilt die and cutter (page 13)

Template plastic or paper (if using patterns)

CUTTING

WOF = width of fabric

FROM WHITE SOLID FABRIC:
- Cut 8 strips 1½" (3.8 cm) × WOF. From 6 strips, cut 54 strips 1½" × 4" (3.8 × 10 cm). From the remaining 2 strips, cut 18 rectangles 1½" × 3" (3.8 × 7.5 cm).
- Cut 3 strips 5" (12.5 cm) × WOF. From the strips, cut 18 squares 5" × 5" (12.5 × 12.5 cm). Cut 1 piece A from each square.

FROM BLUE SOLID FABRIC:
- Cut 2 strips 3" (7.5 cm) × WOF. From 1 strip, cut 10 rectangles 3" × 4" (7.5 × 10 cm). From the second strip, cut 6 rectangles 3" × 4" (7.5 × 10 cm) and 4 squares 3" × 3" (7.5 × 7.5 cm) for a total of 16 rectangles 3" × 4" (7.5 × 10 cm) and 4 squares 3" × 3" (7.5 × 7.5 cm).
- Cut 1 strip 1½" (3.8 cm) × WOF. Cut 4 strips 1½" × 4" (3.8 × 10 cm) and 2 rectangles 1½" × 3" (3.8 × 7.5 cm).
- Cut 1 strip 4" (10 cm) × WOF. Cut 4

continued on the next page >

the pattern

LOOSELY CURVED WALL HANGING

the mix

Drunkard's Path units combine with super simple squares and strips to make a unique blend.

Here is fabulously fashionable wall art of the best-quilted kind. This is the perfect project to get your curved piecing feet wet. Much more than just a splash, these bold pools of color dance graphically on this wall quilt. Making it in bright solids gives it plenty of punch. Choose your favorite palette, start stitching, and end up with a wonderfully gratifying little quilt.

squares 4" × 4" (10 × 10 cm). Cut 1 piece B from each square.

- Cut 1 strip 5" (12.5 cm) × WOF. Cut 2 squares 5" × 5" (12.5 × 12.5 cm). Cut 1 piece A from each square.

FROM ORANGE SOLID FABRIC:
- Cut 1 strip 4" × 22" (10 × 56 cm). Cut 4 squares 4" × 4" (10 × 10 cm). Cut 1 piece B from each square.
- Cut 2 strips 3" × 22" (7.5 × 56 cm). From 1 strip, cut 1 rectangle 3" × 4" (7.5 × 10 cm) and 4 squares 3" × 3" (7.5 × 7.5 cm). From the second strip, cut 5 rectangles 3" × 4" (7.5 × 10 cm) for a total of 6 rectangles 3" × 4" (7.5 × 10 cm) and 4 squares 3" × 3" (7.5 × 7.5 cm).

FROM RED SOLID FABRIC:
- Cut 1 strip 4" × 22" (10 × 56 cm). Cut 4 squares 4" × 4" (10 × 10 cm). Cut 1 piece B from each square.
- Cut 3 strips 3" × 22" (7.5 × 56 cm). From 1 strip, cut 1 rectangle 3" × 4" (7.5 × 10 cm) and 4 squares 3" × 3" (7.5 × 7.5 cm). From the second strip, cut 5 rectangles 3" × 4" (7.5 × 10 cm) for a total of 6 rectangles 3" × 4" (7.5 × 10 cm) and 4 squares 3" × 3" (7.5 × 7.5 cm).

FROM LIME GREEN SOLID FABRIC:
- Cut 1 strip 4" × 22" (10 × 56 cm). Cut 4 squares 4" × 4" (10 × 10 cm). Cut 1 piece B from each square.
- Cut 1 strip 3" × 22" (7.5 × 56 cm). Cut 2 rectangles 3" × 4" (7.5 × 10 cm) and 4 squares 3" × 3" (7.5 × 7.5 cm).

FROM PURPLE SOLID FABRIC:
- Cut 1 strip 4" × 22" (10 × 56 cm). Cut 4 squares 4" × 4" (10 × 10 cm). Cut 1 piece B from each square.
- Cut 3 strips 3" × 22" (7.5 × 56 cm). From 2 strips, cut 4 rectangles 3" × 4" (7.5 × 10 cm) for a total of 8 rectangles 3" × 4" (7.5 × 10 cm). From the third strip, cut 4 squares 3" × 3" (7.5 × 7.5 cm).

FROM BACKING FABRIC:
Cut 1 piece 39" (99 cm) × WOF.

FROM BINDING FABRIC:
Cut 4 strips 2½" (6.5 cm) × WOF.

MAKING THE BLOCKS

Unfinished block size: 4" × 4" (10 × 10 cm)
This quilt is put together in sections, each composed of a different number and arrangement of blocks.

1 Sew together all the pieces A and B as follows **(fig. 1)**:
- Sew 4 white solid pieces A to 4 blue solid pieces B.
- Sew 4 white solid pieces A to 4 orange solid pieces B.
- Sew 2 white solid pieces A to 2 lime green solid pieces B.
- Sew 4 white solid pieces A to 4 red solid pieces B.
- Sew 4 white solid pieces A to 4 purple solid pieces B.
- Sew 2 blue solid pieces A to 2 lime green solid pieces B.

Press all seams toward piece B. You will have a total of twenty quarter-circle units 4" × 4" (10 × 10 cm).

2 To each solid color rectangle 3" × 4" (7.5 × 10 cm), sew a strip 1½" × 4" (3.8 × 10 cm) along the 4" (10 cm) side **(fig. 2)** as follows:
- Sew 14 blue solid rectangles to white solid strips.
- Sew 2 lime green solid rectangles to blue solid strips.
- Sew 6 orange solid rectangles to white solid strips.
- Sew 8 purple solid rectangles to white solid strips.
- Sew 6 red solid rectangles to white solid strips.

Press all seams away from the small strip.

3 To each solid color square 3" × 3" (7.5 × 7.5 cm), sew a strip 1½" × 3" (3.8 × 7.5 cm) along one side. Press the seam away from the strip. Sew a strip 1½" × 4" (3.8 × 10 cm) as shown **(fig. 3)**. Sew as follows:

- Sew 4 blue solid squares to white solid strips.

- Sew 2 lime green solid squares to blue solid strips.

- Sew 2 lime green solid squares to white solid strips.

- Sew 4 orange solid squares to white solid strips.

- Sew 4 purple solid squares to white solid strips.

- Sew 4 red solid squares to white solid strips.

Press the seams away from the small strip.

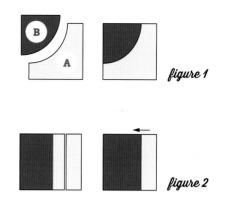

figure 1

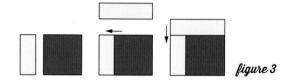

figure 2

figure 3

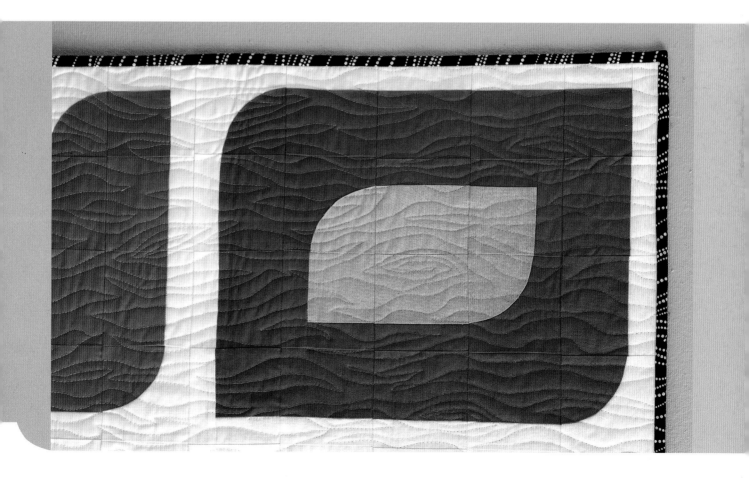

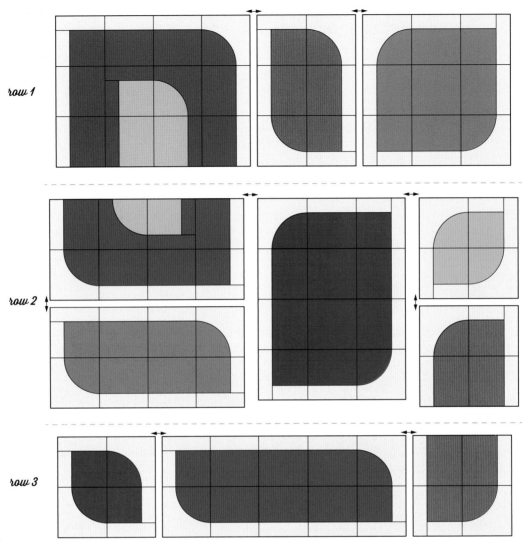

row 1

row 2

row 3

LOOSELY CURVED CONSTRUCTION DIAGRAM

MAKING THE QUILT TOP

1 Lay out the quilt blocks as shown in the Loosely Curved Construction Diagram. There are 11 sections of various sizes:

- 2 lime green/ blue/white

- 1 blue/white

- 2 red/white

- 3 orange/white

- 2 purple/white

- 1 lime green/white

2 Sew together each color block section, placing the three different types of blocks as shown in the diagram. Press seams in one direction.

3 Sew the finished sections together to create three rows. Sew the rows together, matching adjacent seams. Press the seams open.

FINISHING

1 Refer to Finishing Your Quilt (page 132) or use your favorite methods to layer and baste the wall hanging top, batting, and backing.

2 Quilt as desired. Take advantage of the small scale of this wall hanging to try a more labor-intensive quilting technique such as the wood grain I did here. Other great options are pebble quilting or swirls.

3 Bind your wall hanging using my French double-fold binding method as described in Binding (page 139) or your own preferred method. If desired, use your favorite method to add a sleeve on the back for hanging.

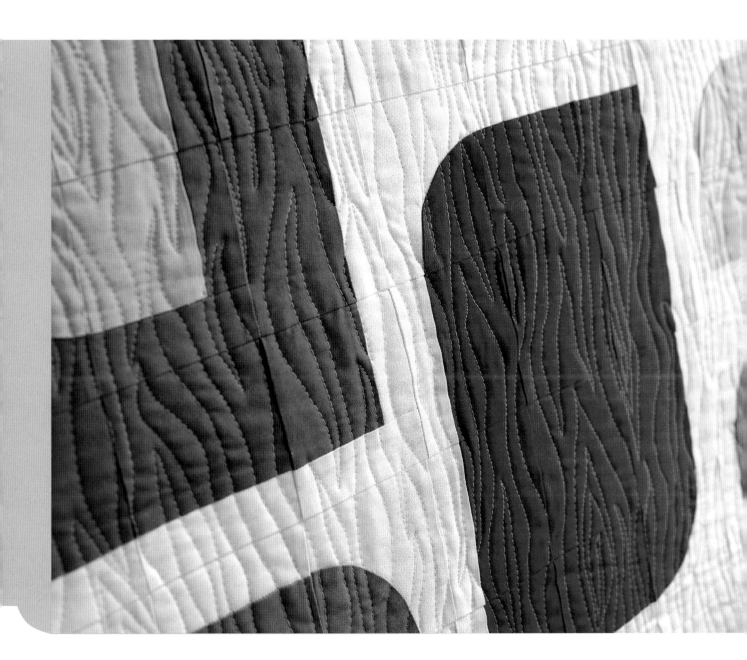

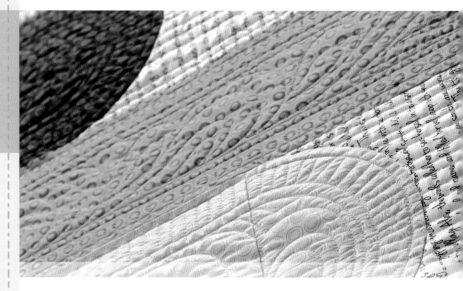

finished size
84" × 94" (213 × 229 cm)

designed and pieced by
ANGELA PINGEL

quilted by
KRISTA WITHERS

MATERIALS

Fabric amounts are based on yardage with a usable width of 42" (106.5 cm). Fabric amounts are also based on non-pieced long strips. This will yield a generous amount of extra fabric to use in another project.

¾ yd (68.5 cm) red print fabric

1⅛ yd (102 cm) orange print fabric

1¾ yd (1.6 m) lime green print fabric

2⅛ yd (1.9 m) teal print fabric

1¼ yd (114.5 cm) navy blue print fabric

1½ yd (137 cm) gray print fabric

4¼ yd (4 m) text print fabric

7¾ yd (7 m) backing fabric

¾ yd (68.5 cm) binding fabric

92" × 102" (234 × 259 cm) batting

TOOLS

Template patterns M, N, O, and P

Template plastic or paper

CUTTING

WOF = width of fabric; LOF = length of fabric

All pieces are cut LOF, unless otherwise specified. Remember, if you find it easier, cut fabric squares before cutting out the Drunkard's Path pieces.

FROM RED PRINT FABRIC:
• Cut 1 strip 6½" × 24" (16.5 × 61 cm).
• Cut 2 pieces N.

FROM ORANGE PRINT FABRIC:
• Cut 1 strip 6½" × 35½" (16.5 × 90 cm).
• Cut 1 strip 6½" × 15" (16.5 × 38 cm).
• Cut 1 strip 9½" × 38½" (24 × 96.5 cm).
• Cut 2 pieces N, 2 pieces M, and 2 pieces P.

continued on the next page >

the pattern

PAINT
DRIPS
QUILT

the mix
Long pours of color end in wide curves for a delicious rainbow effect.

Can't you just feel the paint slipping down the walls with this design? This quilt would also be beautiful in monochromatic tones—perhaps blues to represent water droplets. Picture this quilt on a teenager's bed, and you will see one very happy teenager! (And who doesn't want that?)

Long strips of high-contrast fabrics are very effective against a neutral text print background. The small-scale prints read as solids from a distance, creating texture.

FROM LIME GREEN PRINT FABRIC:
- Cut 1 strip 6½" × 60" (16.5 × 152.5 cm).
- Cut 1 strip 6½" × 26½" (16.5 × 67.5 cm).
- Cut 1 strip 9½" × 29½" (24 × 75 cm).
- Cut 1 strip 3½" × 18" (9 × 45.5 cm).
- Cut 2 pieces N, 4 pieces M, and 6 pieces P.

FROM TEAL PRINT FABRIC:
- Cut 1 strip 6½" × 73½" (16.5 × 186.7 cm) LOF.
- Cut 2 pieces N.

FROM NAVY BLUE PRINT FABRIC:
- Cut 1 strip 9½" × 40½" (24 × 103 cm).
- Cut 2 pieces P.

FROM GRAY PRINT FABRIC:
- Cut 1 strip 9½" × 26½" (24 × 67.5 cm).
- Cut 1 strip 6½" × 15" (16.5 × 38 cm).
- Cut 1 strip 6½" × 50" (16.5 × 127 cm).
- Cut 2 pieces P, 2 pieces M, and 2 pieces N.

FROM TEXT PRINT FABRIC:
- Cut 1 rectangle 78" (198 cm) × WOF and 1 rectangle 68" (173 cm) × WOF. Refer to the Text Print Cutting Diagrams to cut the following pieces (note orientation if using a one-way print):
  » 1 strip 6½" × 67¾" (16.5 × 172 cm)
  » 1 strip 6½" × 56¾" (16.5 × 144 cm)
  » 1 strip 6½" × 77" (16.5 × 196 cm)
  » 1 strip 9½" × 2" (24 × 5 cm)
  » 1 strip 9½" × 64¾" (24 × 164.5 cm)
  » 1 strip 6½" × 77¼" (16.5 × 196 cm)
  » 1 strip 9½" × 52¼" (24 × 132.5 cm)
  » 1 strip 6½" × 32¼" (16.5 × 82 cm)
  » 1 strip 9½" × 33¾" (24 × 85.5 cm)
  » 1 strip 6½" × 15" (16.5 × 38 cm)
  » 1 strip 6½" × 18¾" (16.5 × 48 cm)
  » 1 strip 9½" × 50¼" (24 × 127.5 cm)
  » 1 strip 6½" × 66¼" (16.5 × 168c m)
  » 1 strip 6½" × 42¼" (16.5 × 108 cm)
  » Cut 10 pieces M, 8 pieces N, and 12 pieces O.

FROM BACKING FABRIC:
- Cut 3 rectangles 92" (234 cm) × WOF.

FROM BINDING FABRIC:
- Cut 9 strips 2½" (6.5 cm) × WOF.

TIP

When cutting long lengths of fabric, roughly over-measure, and cut a snip at the edge of the fabric. Rip the fabric at the snip, and press the ripped edge flat. Then rotary cut to size. Because you have over-measured your yardage, you will be able to cut away any of the area where the fabric's weave may have been distorted by ripping.

MAKING THE QUILT TOP

This quilt is assembled in twelve columns, which are then sewn together to complete the quilt top.

QUARTER-CIRCLE UNITS

Begin by making the quarter-circle units for all the columns.

1 Sew together the small curved pieces M and N **(fig. 1)** as follows:

- Sew 2 text print pieces M to 2 red print pieces N.
- Sew 2 text print pieces M to 2 orange print pieces N.

figure 1

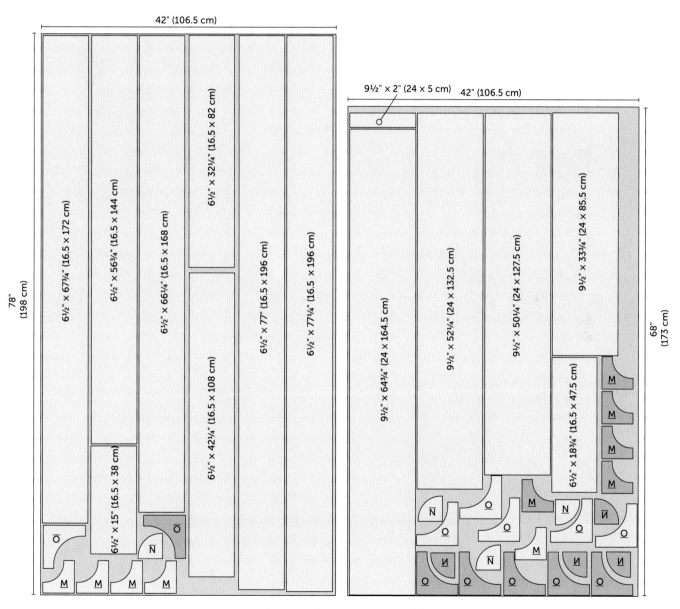

42" (106.5 cm)

78" (198 cm)

6½" × 67¾" (16.5 × 172 cm)

6½" × 56¾" (16.5 × 144 cm)

6½" × 66¼" (16.5 × 168 cm)

6½" × 32¼" (16.5 × 82 cm)

6½" × 42¼" (16.5 × 108 cm)

6½" × 77" (16.5 × 196 cm)

6½" × 77¼" (16.5 × 196 cm)

6½" × 15" (16.5 × 38 cm)

Ō

N̄

M   M   M   M

9½" × 2" (24 × 5 cm)

42" (106.5 cm)

68" (173 cm)

9½" × 64¾" (24 × 164.5 cm)

9½" × 52¼" (24 × 132.5 cm)

9½" × 50¼" (24 × 127.5 cm)

9½" × 33¾" (24 × 85.5 cm)

6½" × 18¾" (16.5 × 47.5 cm)

M
M
M
M

N̄   O   M   N̄

O   O   O

O   O   O   N̄

N̄   N   N   N

O   O   O   O

TEXT PRINT CUTTING DIAGRAMS

TIP

If you are using directional prints, pay careful attention to left- and right-oriented curves. Cut your pattern pieces accordingly. The curved pieces need to be cut the same direction as any adjacent strips.

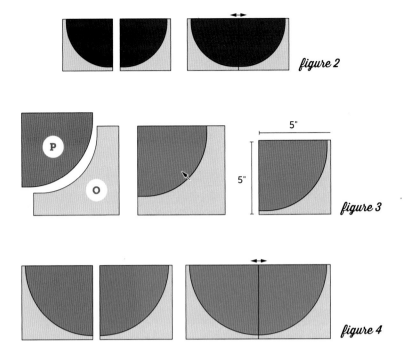

figure 2

figure 3

figure 4

- Sew 2 orange print pieces M to 2 text print pieces N.
- Sew 2 text print pieces M to 2 lime green print pieces N.
- Sew 4 lime green print pieces M to 4 text print pieces N.
- Sew 2 text print pieces M to 2 teal print pieces N.
- Sew 2 gray print pieces M to 2 text print pieces N.
- Sew 2 text print pieces M to 2 gray print pieces N.

Press the seams toward piece N. Trim each unit to 3½" x 3½" (9 x 9 cm) leaving a ¼" (6 mm) seam allowance on the M piece **(fig. 1)**. You will have a total of eighteen quarter-circle units.

2 Sew the units from Step 1 into matching pairs to make nine half-circle units **(fig. 2)**. Press all seams open.

3 Sew together large curved pieces O and P **(fig. 3)** as follows:

- Sew 2 text print pieces O to 2 orange print pieces P.
- Sew 6 text print pieces O to 6 lime green print pieces P.
- Sew 2 text print pieces O to 2 navy print pieces P.
- Sew 2 text print pieces O to 2 gray print pieces P.

Press the seams toward piece P. Trim each unit to 5" x 5" (12.5 x 12.5 cm) leaving a ¼" (6 mm) seam allowance on the O pieces **(fig. 3)**.

4 Sew the units from Step 3 into matching pairs to make six half-circle blocks **(fig. 4)**. Press all seams open.

MAKING THE COLUMNS

Assemble each of the twelve vertical columns of the quilt in order from left to right. Refer to the Paint Drips Construction Diagram for the correct orientation of the half-circle blocks.

1 To make Column 1, sew the red print strip 6½" x 24" (16.5 x 61 cm) to the top of the red/text print half-circle block and the text print strip 6½" x 67¾" (16.5 x 172 cm) to the bottom.

2 To make Column 2, sew the orange print strip 6½" x 35½" (16.5 x 90 cm) to the top of the small orange/text print half-circle block and the text print strip 6½" x 56¾" (16.5 x 144 cm) to the bottom.

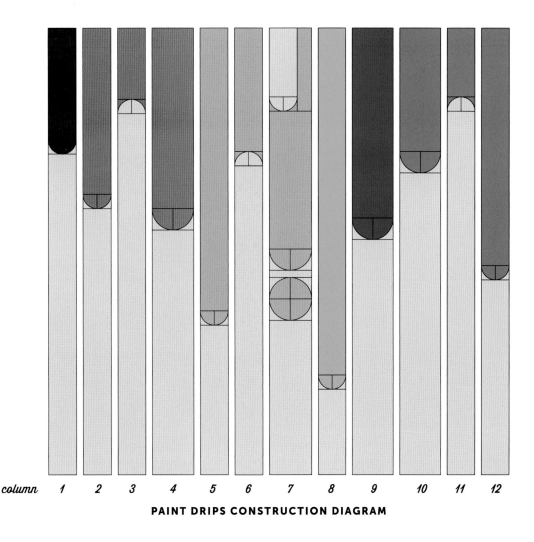

column   1   2   3   4   5   6   7   8   9   10   11   12

PAINT DRIPS CONSTRUCTION DIAGRAM

3 To make Column 3, sew the orange print strip 6½" × 15" (16.5 × 38 cm) to the top of the small text print/orange half-circle block and the text print strip 6½" × 77" (16.5 × 196 cm) to the bottom.

4 To make Column 4, sew the orange print strip 9½" × 38½" (24 × 98 cm) to the top of the large orange/text print half-circle block and the text print strip 9½" × 52¼" (24 × 132.5 cm) to the bottom.

5 To make Column 5, sew the lime green print strip 6½" × 60" (16.5 × 152.5 cm) to the top of the small lime green/text print half-circle block and the text print strip 6½" × 32¼" (16.5 × 82 cm) to the bottom.

6 To make Column 6, sew the text print strip 6½" × 26½" (16.5 × 67.5 cm) to the top of the small text print/lime green print half-circle block and the text print strip 6½" × 66¼" (16.5 × 168 cm) to the bottom.

7 To make Column 7, refer to **Figure 5** (page 104). Sew the text print strip 6½" × 15" (16.5 × 38 cm) to the small text print/lime green print half-circle block. Then sew the lime green print strip 3½" × 18" (9 × 45.5 cm) to the right side. Sew the lime green print strip 9½" × 29½" (24 × 75 cm) to the top of a large lime green/text print half-circle block. Sew the text print strip 9½" × 2" (24 × 5 cm) to the bottom. Sew the two remaining large lime green/text print half-circle blocks together to make a circle. Sew this

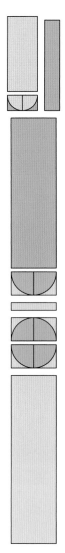

figure 5

circle block to the top of the text print strip 9½" × 33¾" (24 × 85.5 cm). Sew together all three pieces to complete Column 7.

8 To make Column 8, sew the teal print strip 6½" × 73½" (16.5 × 186.7 cm) to the top of the small teal/text print half-circle block and the text print strip 6½" × 18¾" (16.5 × 48 cm) to the bottom.

9 To make Column 9, sew the navy print strip 9½" × 40½" (24 × 103 cm) to the top of the large navy print half-circle block and the text print strip 9½" × 50¼" (24 × 127.5 cm) to the bottom.

10 To make Column 10, sew the gray print strip 9½" × 26½" (24 × 67.5 cm) to the top of the large gray/text print half-circle block and the text print strip 9½" × 64¾" (24 × 164.5 cm) to the bottom.

11 To make Column 11, sew the gray print strip 6½" × 15" (16.5 × 38 cm) to the top of the small text print/gray print half-circle block and the text print strip 6½" × 77¼" (16.5 × 196 cm) to the bottom.

12 To make Column 12, sew the gray print strip 6½" × 50" (16.5 × 127 cm) to the top of the small gray/text print half-circle block and the text print strip 6½" × 42¼" (16.5 × 108 cm) to the bottom.

ASSEMBLY AND FINISHING

1 Sew together columns 1 through 12 in order from left to right to complete your quilt top. Because of the long seams, you may need to trim the quilt's lower edge even after stitching, as some strips may have shifted slightly.

2 Refer to Finishing Your Quilt (page 132) or use your favorite methods to layer and baste the quilt top, batting, and backing.

3 Quilt as desired. This quilt has channel quilting on the background. Longarm quilter Krista Withers created a variety of patterns on the drips, along with wonderful droplet motifs for the background areas.

4 Bind your quilt using my French double-fold binding method as described in binding (page 139) or your own preferred method.

finished size
60" × 70" (152.5 × 178 cm)

designed and pieced by
ANGELA PINGEL

quilted by
KELLY BOWSER & ANGELA PINGEL

MATERIALS

Fabric amounts are based on yardage with a usable width of 42" (106.5 cm). Fat quarters are 18" × 22" (45.5 × 56 cm).

3¼ yd (3 m) yellow print fabric

8 fat quarters of assorted green print fabrics

4 fat quarters of assorted purple print fabrics

¼ yd (23 cm) brown print fabric

4 yd (3.7 m) backing fabric

⅝ yd (57 cm) binding fabric

68" × 78" (173 × 198 cm) batting

TOOLS

Template patterns G and H

Template plastic or paper

CUTTING

WOF = width of fabric

FROM YELLOW PRINT FABRIC:

- Cut 9 strips 5" (12.5 cm) × WOF. Cut 8 squares 5" × 5" from each strip for a total of 72 squares. Cut 1 piece G from each square.

- Cut 1 piece 61½" (156 cm) × WOF. Refer to the Mod Garden Cutting Diagram (page 108) to cut it into the following:

  » 1 strip 10½" × 60½" (26.5 × 153.5 cm)

  » 4 strips 3½" × 30½" (9 × 77.5 cm)

  » 12 rectangles 5½" × 10½" (14 × 26.5 cm)

  » 30 strips 2½" × 8½" (6.5 × 21.5 cm)

FROM EACH OF 4 GREEN PRINT FABRICS:

- Cut 3 strips 4½" × 22" (11.5 × 56 cm). Cut 4 squares 4½" × 4½" (11.5 × 11.5 cm) from each strip for a total of 48 squares.

continued on the next page >

the pattern

MOD
GARDEN
LAP QUILT

the mix

Leaves muddled together in liquid gold with a berry garnish, showing off what simple curves and squares can do

As soon as you start playing with curves and squares, this leaf pattern emerges. Here is my take on the ever-popular stem-and-leaf motif. Highly stylized, this quilt is perfect for those who don't want anything too flowery. Experiment with colors and arrangement to create the piece that is perfect for you!

FROM REMAINING 4 GREEN PRINT FABRICS:

• Cut 3 strips 4½" × 22" (11.5 × 56 cm). Cut 4 squares 4½" × 4½" (11.5 × 11.5 cm) from each strip for a total of 48 squares. Cut 1 piece H from each square.

FROM EACH PURPLE PRINT FABRIC:

• Cut 2 strips 4½" × 22" (11.5 × 56 cm). Cut 24 squares 4½" × 4½" (11.5 × 11.5 cm) from the assorted strips. Cut 1 piece H from each square.

FROM BROWN PRINT FABRIC:

• Cut 3 strips 2½" (6.5 cm) × WOF. From each strip, cut 2 strips 2½" × 20½" (6.5 × 52 cm) for a total of 6 strips.

FROM BACKING FABRIC:

• Cut 2 rectangles 68" (173 cm) × WOF.

FROM BINDING FABRIC:

• Cut 7 strips 2½" (6.5 cm) × WOF.

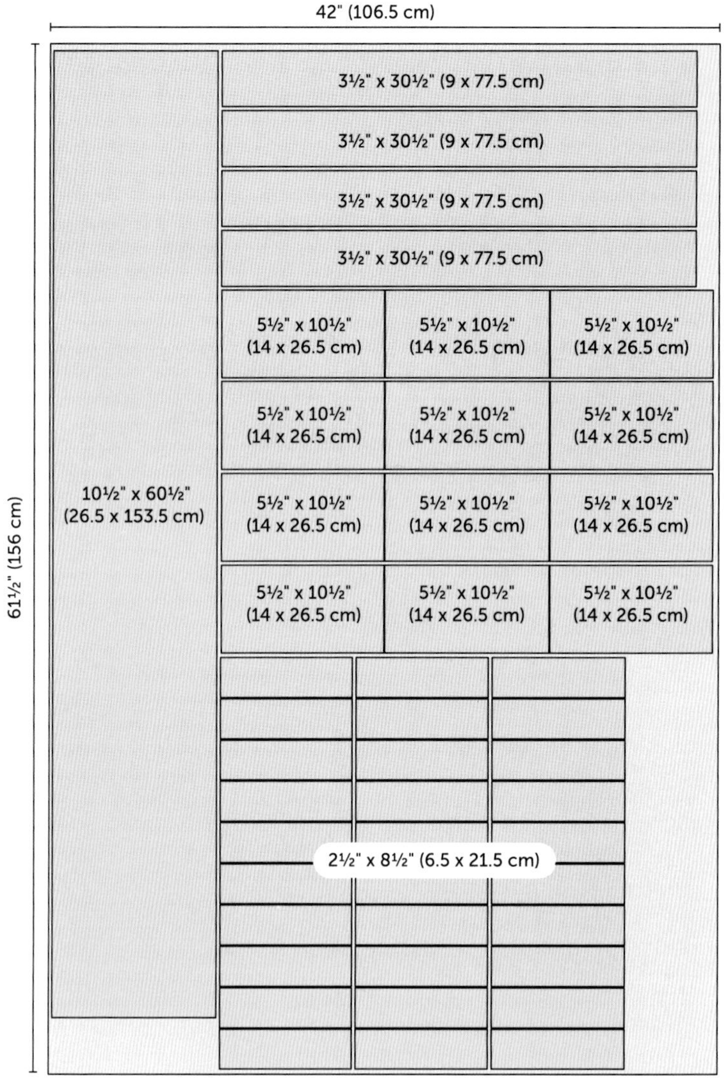

42" (106.5 cm)

61½" (156 cm)

10½" x 60½" (26.5 x 153.5 cm)	3½" x 30½" (9 x 77.5 cm)
	3½" x 30½" (9 x 77.5 cm)
	3½" x 30½" (9 x 77.5 cm)
	3½" x 30½" (9 x 77.5 cm)

5½" x 10½" (14 x 26.5 cm)	5½" x 10½" (14 x 26.5 cm)	5½" x 10½" (14 x 26.5 cm)
5½" x 10½" (14 x 26.5 cm)	5½" x 10½" (14 x 26.5 cm)	5½" x 10½" (14 x 26.5 cm)
5½" x 10½" (14 x 26.5 cm)	5½" x 10½" (14 x 26.5 cm)	5½" x 10½" (14 x 26.5 cm)
5½" x 10½" (14 x 26.5 cm)	5½" x 10½" (14 x 26.5 cm)	5½" x 10½" (14 x 26.5 cm)

2½" x 8½" (6.5 x 21.5 cm)

MOD GARDEN CUTTING DIAGRAM

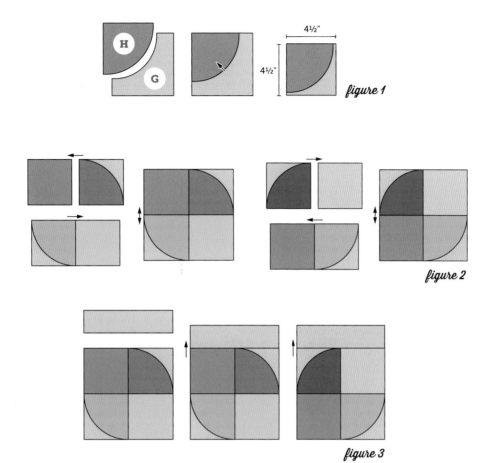

figure 1

figure 2

figure 3

MAKING THE BLOCKS

Unfinished block size: 18½" × 30½" (47 × 77.5 cm)
This quilt has twenty-four leaf blocks and six flower blocks.

QUARTER-CIRCLE UNITS

1   Sew together curved pieces G and H **(fig. 1)**. Sew forty-eight yellow print pieces G to forty-eight green print pieces H. Press the seams toward H. Sew twenty-four yellow print pieces A to twenty-four purple print pieces H. Press the seams toward H.

2   Trim all quarter-circle units to 4½" × 4½" (11.5 × 11.5 cm) with a ¼" (6 mm) seam allowance on piece G.

LEAF BLOCKS

1   Assemble the leaf blocks using the green/yellow quarter-circle units. Each leaf block is composed of two yellow/green units and two green squares 4½" × 4½" (11.5 × 11.5 cm). Orient the pieces left or right and mix up the fabrics, as shown in **Figure 2**. Sew the pairs of units together, and press the seams toward the squares.

2   Sew together the top and bottom units of each block **(fig. 2)**. Nest the seam allowances at the center point. Press the seams open. You will have a total of twenty-four leaf blocks.

3   Sew a yellow strip 2½" × 8½" (6.5 × 21.5 cm) to the top of each leaf block **(fig. 3)**. Press the seams toward the yellow strips.

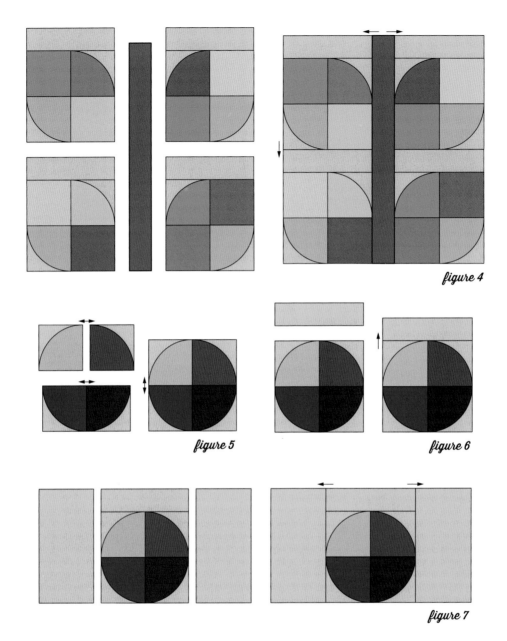

figure 4

figure 5

figure 6

figure 7

4 Sew the leaf blocks together in pairs as shown **(fig. 4)**. Sew six sets of left leaf blocks and six sets of right leaf blocks. Press the seams toward the yellow strips.

5 Sew opposite facing leaf blocks to either side of a brown strip 2½" × 20½" (6.5 × 52 cm) **(fig. 4)**. Press the seams toward the brown strip.

FLOWER BLOCKS

1 Assemble the flower units in pairs, using the purple/yellow quarter-circle units you made earlier. Orient the units as shown **(fig. 5)**, and sew them together. Press the seams open.

2 Sew together the top and bottom pairs, matching adjacent seams. Press the seams open.

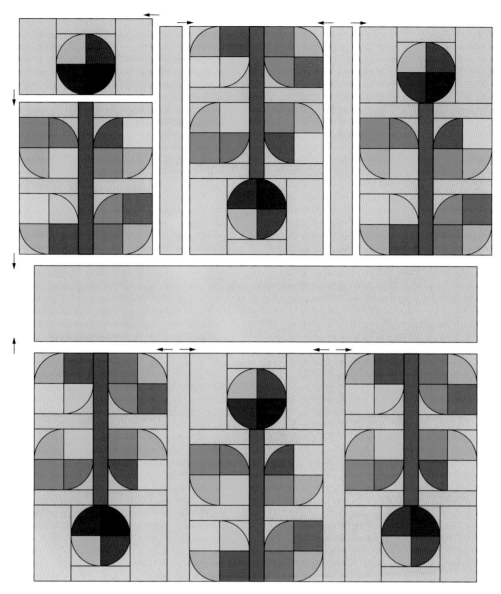

MOD GARDEN CONSTRUCTION DIAGRAM

3 Sew a yellow strip 2½" × 8½" (6.5 × 21.5 cm) to the top of each purple circle block **(fig. 6)**. Press the seams toward the yellow strips.

4 Sew a yellow rectangle 5½" × 10½" (14 × 26.5 cm) to either side of the purple circle block **(fig. 7)**. Press the seams toward the yellow strips. You will have a total of six flower blocks.

MAKING THE QUILT TOP

1 Refer to the Mod Garden Construction Diagram to sew together the six flower blocks and six leaf blocks. Press the seams toward the leaf blocks.

2 Assemble the flower/leaf sections into two rows, oriented as shown in the Mod Garden Construction Diagram (page 111). Sew a yellow strip 3½" × 30½" (9 × 77.5 cm) between the sections. Press the seams toward the yellow strips.

3 Refer to the diagram to assemble the full quilt top. Sew the yellow rectangle 10½" × 60½" (26.5 × 153.5 cm) between the two flower/leaf rows. Press the seams toward the yellow pieces.

FINISHING

1 Refer to Finishing Your Quilt (page 132) or use your favorite methods to layer and baste the quilt top, batting, and backing.

2 Quilt as desired. Quilter Kelly Bowser quilted an overall swirling vine pattern on the background. On the purple flowers, I stitched concentric circles, and on the leaves, I stitched a leaf design.

3 Bind your quilt using my French double-fold binding method as described in Binding (page 139) or your own preferred method.

TIP

You can make some simple changes to this quilt pattern to give it a whole different look and feel. Try using just the leaf and stem to create a continuous running pattern up and down the quilt. Or just use one column and create a table runner or wall hanging. Also, don't be afraid to change the color of the "leaves." Aqua, red, and peach are just some of the interesting alternatives to consider.

finished size
68" x 84" (173 x 213 cm)

designed and pieced by
ANGELA PINGEL

quilted by
KRISTA WITHERS

MATERIALS

Fabric amounts are based on yardage with a usable width of 42" (106.5 cm). A charm square is 5" × 5" (12.5 × 12.5 cm).

12 assorted fuchsia charm squares

12 assorted aqua charm squares

12 assorted red charm squares

10 assorted green charm squares

10 assorted yellow charm squares

5½ yd (5 m) black linen fabric

5¼ yd (4.8 m) backing fabric

⅔ yd (61 cm) binding fabric

76" × 92" (193 × 234 cm) batting

TOOLS

Template patterns G and H for the large units, and Q and R for the small units

Template plastic or paper

CUTTING

WOF = width of fabric

FROM FUCHSIA CHARM SQUARES:
- From each of 4 squares, cut 1 piece G. From each of 4 squares, cut 1 piece H.

FROM AQUA CHARM SQUARES:
- From each of 4 squares, cut 1 piece G. From each of 4 squares, cut 1 piece H.

FROM RED CHARM SQUARES:
- From each of 4 squares, cut 1 piece G. From each of 4 squares, cut 1 piece H.

FROM GREEN CHARM SQUARES:
- Cut a square 4½" × 4½" (11.5 × 11.5 cm) from each of 10 charm squares. From each of 4 squares, cut 1 piece Q. From each of 4 squares, cut 1 piece H.

continued on the next page >

the pattern

ORNAMENTAL QUILT

the mix

Bright orbs of color pop in a pool of velvet black; curves shape themselves into classic ogee designs that are truly ornamental.

This quilt is designed to use those special charm squares of fabric you've been hoarding. Showcase your favorite fabrics in a minimalist, but never boring, design of curves. A background of solid or solid-like fabric contrasts well with the colors of the charms. Monochromatic fabrics or tone-on-tone fabrics best show the beautiful curves of the ornament motifs.

FROM YELLOW CHARM SQUARES:
- Cut a square 4½" × 4½" (11.5 × 11.5 cm) from each of 10 charm squares. From each of 4 squares, cut 1 piece Q. From each of 4 squares, cut 1 piece H.

FROM BLACK LINEN FABRIC:
- Cut 8 strips 16½" (42 cm) × WOF. From the strips, cut 15 squares 16½" × 16½" (42 × 42 cm).
- Cut 4 strips 5" (12.5 cm) × WOF. From the strips, cut 32 squares 5" × 5" (12.5 × 12.5 cm). From the squares, cut 20 pieces G and 12 pieces H.
- Cut 3 strips 4½" (11.5 cm) × WOF. Cut the strips into 20 squares 4½" × 4½" (11.5 × 11.5 cm).
- Cut 11 strips 2½" (6.5 cm) × WOF.
  » From 2 strips, cut 4 strips 2½" × 16½" (6.5 × 42 cm).
  » From 1 strip, cut 4 rectangles 2½" × 4½" (6.5 × 11.5 cm) and 8 squares 2½" × 2½" (6.5 × 6.5 cm). Cut 1 piece R from each square.
- Use the remaining 8 strips for the borders.

FROM BACKING FABRIC:
- Cut 2 rectangles 92" (234 cm) × WOF.

FROM BINDING FABRIC:
- Cut 8 strips 2½" (6.5 cm) × WOF.

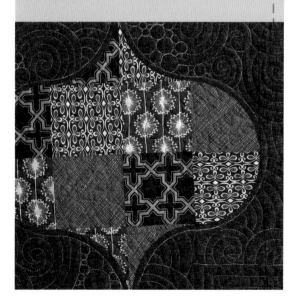

MAKING THE BLOCKS

This quilt has three large and two small orb blocks.

LARGE ORB BLOCKS

Unfinished block size: 16½" × 16½" (42 × 42 cm)
Make three blocks, one each of fuchsia, red, and aqua.

1 Sew together curved pieces G and H **(fig. 1)**. Sew four black linen pieces G to four fuchsia pieces H. Sew four fuchsia pieces G to four black linen pieces H. Press the seams toward piece H. Trim the unit to 4½" × 4½" (11.5 × 11.5 cm), leaving a ¼" (6 mm) seam allowance on G **(fig. 2)**. You will have a total of eight fuchsia/black quarter-circle units.

2 Repeat Step 1 to make eight quarter-circle units in red/black and eight units in aqua/black.

3 Assemble each of the three blocks in four rows of four units **(fig. 3)**. Use four black linen squares 4½" × 4½" (11.5 × 11.5 cm), four colored squares 4½" × 4½" (11.5 × 11.5 cm), and the eight quarter-circle units. Press all seams open.

SMALL ORB BLOCKS

Unfinished block size: 16½" × 16½" (42 × 42 cm)
Make two blocks, one each of green and yellow.

1 Sew together curved pieces Q and R **(fig. 4)**. Sew four black linen pieces R to four green pieces Q. Press the seams toward piece R. Trim the Q/R units to 2½" × 2½" (6.5 × 6.5 cm), leaving a ¼" (6 mm) seam allowance on piece Q **(fig. 5)**. You will have a total of four green/black small quarter-circle units. Repeat to make four yellow/black small quarter-circle units. Repeat to make four sets each of black/green and black/yellow G/H units, trimming those to 4½" × 4½" (11.5 × 11.5 cm).

2 Sew two sets of Q/R quarter-circle units together as shown **(fig. 6)**. Press the seams open. Sew one black linen rectangle 2½" × 4½" (6.5 × 11.5 cm) to the long edge of each completed unit, noting the unit orientation. Press the seam toward the black linen rectangle. Sew one black linen square 4½" × 4½" (11.5 × 11.5 cm) to either end of each piece. Press the seams open.

3 Sew one Q/R quarter-circle unit to either side of each 4½" × 4½" (11.5 × 11.5 cm) colored print square, noting the orientation of the curves **(fig. 7)**. Press the seams open.

figure 1

figure 4

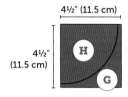
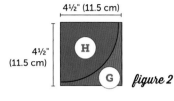

4½" (11.5 cm)

4½" (11.5 cm)

4½" (11.5 cm)

4½" (11.5 cm)

figure 2

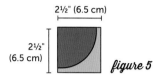

2½" (6.5 cm)

2½" (6.5 cm)

figure 5

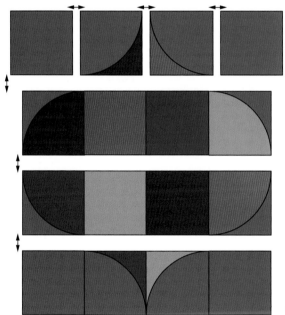

figure 3

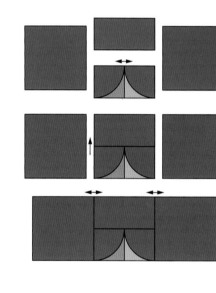

figure 6

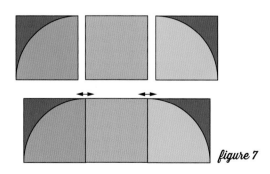

figure 7

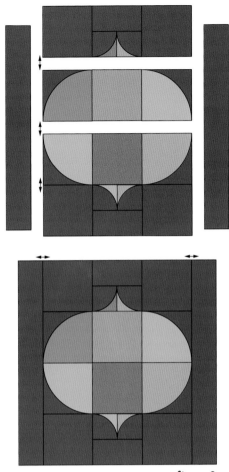

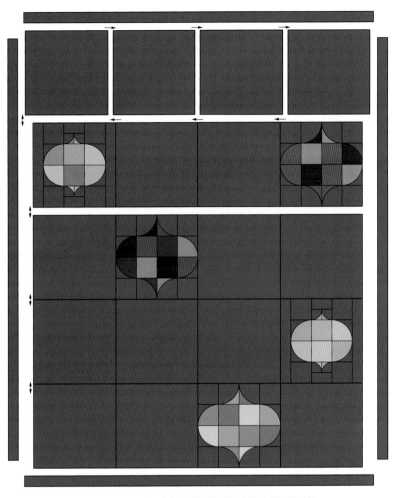

figure 8

ORNAMENTAL CONSTRUCTION DIAGRAM

---

4 Sew the four completed rows together in order, matching adjacent seams **(fig. 8)**. Press the seams open. Sew one black linen strip 2½" × 16½" (6.5 × 42 cm) to either side of the block center. Press the seams toward the black linen fabric.

MAKING THE QUILT TOP

1 Lay out the fifteen black linen blocks 16½" × 16½" (42 × 42 cm) and the large and small pieced orb blocks in five rows of four blocks each, as shown in the Ornamental Construction Diagram. Sew the blocks into rows. Press the seams in one direction, alternating by row. Sew together the rows matching adjacent seams. Press the seams open.

2 For the side borders, sew together two black linen strips 2½" (6.5 cm) × WOF, and trim to 2½" × 80½" (6.5 × 204.5 cm). Repeat to create a second strip.

3 For the top and bottom borders, sew together two black linen strips 2½" (6.5 cm) × WOF, and trim to 2½" × 68½" (6.5 × 174 cm). Repeat to create a second strip.

4 Sew one strip 2½" × 80½" (6.5 × 204.5 cm) to each side of the quilt top. Press the seams toward the borders. Sew one strip 2½" × 68½" (6.5 × 174 cm) to the quilt top and bottom. Press the seams toward the borders.

FINISHING

1. Refer to Finishing Your Quilt (page 132) or use your favorite methods to layer and baste the quilt top, batting, and backing.

2. Quilt as desired. Longarm quilter Krista Withers dressed up the large areas of negative space with a highly creative mixed pattern of bubbles, swirls, and spiral rectangles. Each ornament is treated to a complex quilting pattern reminiscent of antique ornaments for a Christmas tree.

3. Bind your quilt using my French double-fold binding method as described in Binding (page 139) or your own preferred method.

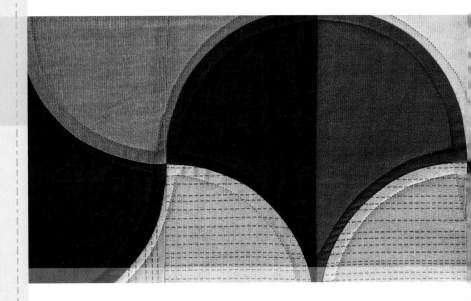

finished size
16" × 40" (40.5 × 101.5 cm)

designed, pieced, and quilted by
ANGELA PINGEL

MATERIALS

Fabric amounts are based on yardage with a usable width of 42" (106.5 cm).

½ yd (45.5 cm) blue solid fabric*

⅜ yd (34.5 cm) yellow solid fabric

⅜ yd (34.5 cm) orange solid fabric

⅝ yd (57 cm) pink solid fabric

⅝ yd (57 cm) purple solid fabric

1¼ yd (114.5 cm) backing fabric

½ yd (45.5 cm) diagonally printed stripe binding fabric

20" × 44" (51 × 112 cm) batting

*I used a near-solid fabric.

TOOLS

Template patterns G and H

Template plastic or paper

CUTTING

WOF = width of fabric

FROM BLUE SOLID FABRIC:
- Cut 2 strips 4½" (11.5 cm) × WOF. Cut 12 squares 4½" × 4½" (11.5 × 11.5 cm). Cut 1 piece H from each square.
- Cut 1 strip 5" (12.5 cm) × WOF. Cut 8 squares 5" × 5" (12.5 × 12.5 cm). Cut 1 piece G from each square.

FROM YELLOW SOLID FABRIC:
- Cut 1 strip 4½" (11.5 cm) × WOF. Cut 4 squares 4½" × 4½" (11.5 × 11.5 cm). Cut 1 piece H from each square.
- Cut 1 strip 5" (12.5 cm) × WOF. Cut 6 squares 5" × 5" (12.5 × 12.5 cm). Cut 1 piece G from each square.

FROM ORANGE SOLID FABRIC:
- Cut 1 strip 4½" (11.5 cm) × WOF. Cut 4 squares 4½" × 4½" (11.5 × 11.5 cm). Cut 1 piece H from each square.
- Cut 1 strip 5" (12.5 cm) × WOF. Cut 6 squares 5" × 5" (12.5 × 12.5 cm). Cut 1 piece G from each square.

continued on the next page >

the pattern
SUNRISE TABLE RUNNER

the mix

A toast to convivial company, created with curves of sunrise colors

Color-blocked solids, interlocking curves, and dynamic back-and-forth movement make this runner a beautiful statement piece for your table. With colors reminiscent of a sunrise, and with curves running in all directions, dinner guests have an optimal view from wherever they're seated. Piece it with accuracy to create a truly seamless design. Moving in and out and up and down, this piece flows with the conversation, as well as your best Cabernet.

FROM PINK SOLID FABRIC:

- Cut 2 strips 4½" (11.5 cm) × WOF. Cut 10 squares 4½" × 4½" (11.5 × 11.5 cm). Cut 1 piece H from each square.
- Cut 2 strips 5" × 5" (12.5 × 12.5 cm) × WOF. Cut 10 squares 5" × 5" (12.5 × 12.5 cm). Cut 1 piece G from each square.

FROM PURPLE SOLID FABRIC:

- Cut 2 strips 4½" (11.5 cm) × WOF. Cut 10 squares 4½" × 4½" (11.5 × 11.5 cm). Cut 1 piece H from each square.
- Cut 2 strips 5" (12.5 cm) × WOF. Cut 10 squares 5" × 5" (12.5 × 12.5 cm). Cut 1 piece G from each square.

FROM BACKING FABRIC:

- Cut 2 strips 20" (51 cm) × WOF.

FROM BINDING FABRIC:

- Cut 3 strips 2½" (6.5 cm) × WOF.

MAKING THE UNITS

Unfinished block size: 4½" × 4½" (11.5 × 11.5 cm)
This runner has forty quarter-circle units.

Sew together curved pieces G and H **(fig. 1)** as follows:

- Sew 6 yellow pieces G to 6 pink pieces H.
- Sew 6 orange pieces G to 6 purple pieces H.
- Sew 6 purple pieces G to 6 blue pieces H.
- Sew 6 pink pieces G to 6 blue pieces H.
- Sew 4 blue pieces G to 4 pink pieces H.
- Sew 4 blue pieces G to 4 purple pieces H.
- Sew 4 pink pieces G to 4 yellow pieces H.
- Sew 4 purple pieces G to 4 orange pieces H.

Press the seams toward piece H. Trim all blocks to 4½" × 4½" (11.5 × 11.5 cm) with a ¼" (6 mm) seam allowance on piece G. Make a total of forty quarter-circle units.

MAKING THE RUNNER

The units for this runner are sewn into five sections.

1 Sections 1, 3, and 5 are identical. Each is composed of eight quarter-circle units. Refer to **Figure 2** for block color placement and orientation. Sew together the units for each section in pairs, and then sew the pairs together, carefully matching adjacent seams. Press all seams open. Make three sections.

2 Sections 2 and 4 are identical. Each is composed of eight quarter-circle units. Refer to **Figure 3** for block color placement and orientation. Sew together the units for each section in pairs, and then sew the pairs together, carefully matching adjacent seams. Press all seams open. Make two sections.

3 Refer to the Sunrise Table Runner Construction Diagram to sew together the table runner sections. First sew together sections 1 and 2. Continue to sew each section to each other until complete, always matching adjacent seams. Press all seams open.

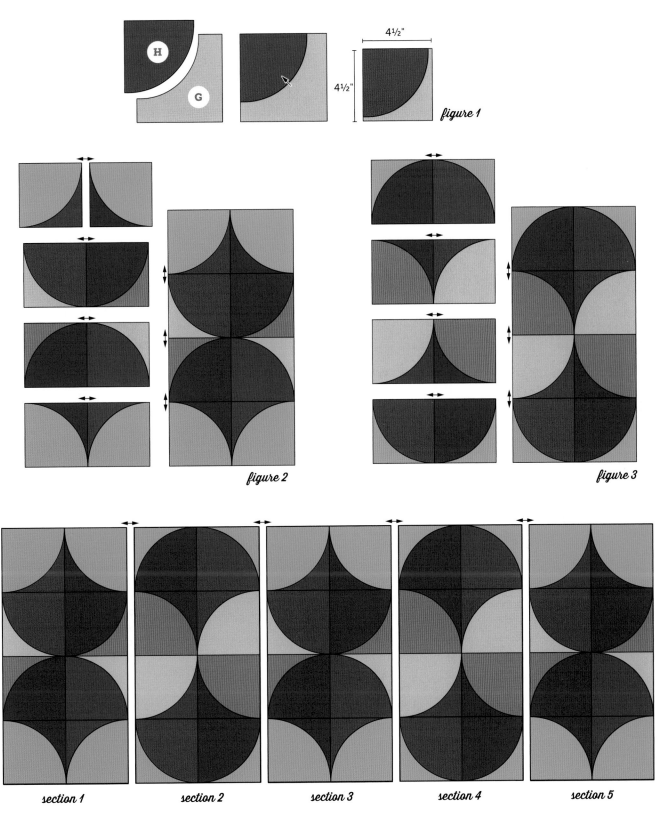

figure 1

4½"

4½"

H

G

figure 2

figure 3

section 1

section 2

section 3

section 4

section 5

SUNRISE TABLE RUNNER CONSTRUCTION DIAGRAM

FINISHING

1   Refer to Finishing Your Quilt (page 132) or use your
    favorite methods to layer and baste the runner top,
    batting, and backing.

2   Quilt as desired. I did simple outline quilting on the
    curves.

3   Bind your runner using my French double-fold bind-
    ing method as described in Binding (page 139) or
    your own preferred method.

TIP

*When sewing on the
binding, make sure not to
cut off the design at the
seam allowance around
the edge!*

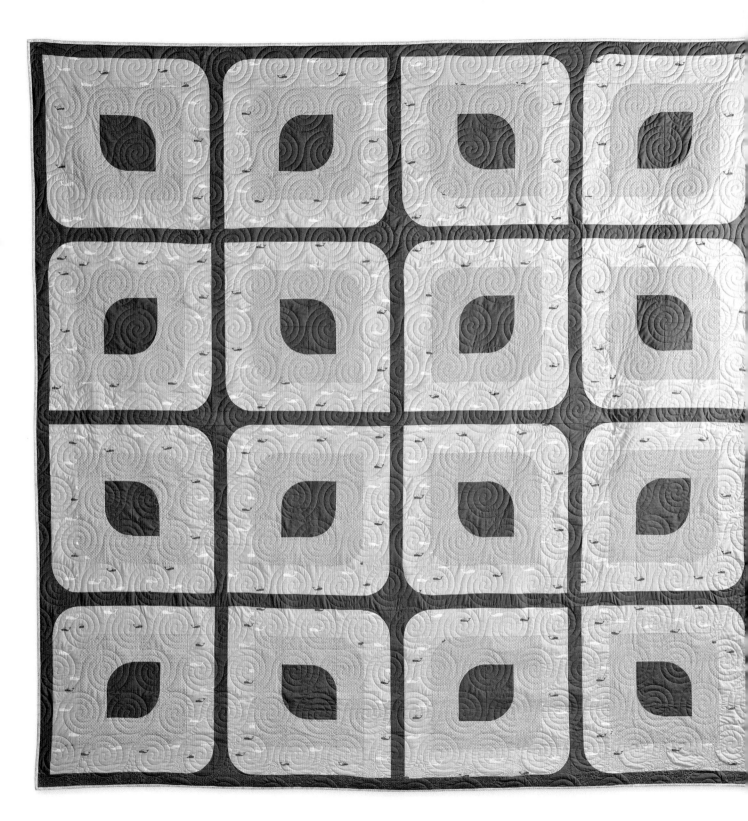

finished size
106" × 106" (269 × 269 cm)

designed and pieced by
ANGELA PINGEL

quilted by
KRISTA WITHERS

pantograph pattern by
PATRICIA RITTER DESIGN

MATERIALS

Fabric amounts are based on yardage with a usable width of 42" (106.5 cm).

5⅓ yd (4.9 m) light blue print fabric

3½ yd (3.2 m) yellow print fabric

4½ yd (4.1 m) gray solid fabric

10 yd (9.2 m) backing fabric

⅞ yd (80 cm) binding fabric

114" × 114" (290 × 290 cm) batting

TOOLS

Template patterns G and H

Template plastic or paper

CUTTING

WOF = width of fabric

FROM LIGHT BLUE PRINT FABRIC:
- Cut 16 strips 4½" (11.5 cm) × WOF. From each strip, cut 2 strips 4½" × 20½" (11.5 × 52 cm) for a total of 32 strips.
- Cut 16 strips 5½" (14 cm) × WOF. From each strip, cut 2 strips 5½" × 16½" (14 × 42 cm) and 2 squares 5" × 5" (12.5 × 12.5 cm) for a total of 32 strips and 32 squares. Cut 1 piece G from each square.
- Cut 4 strips 5" (12.5 cm) × WOF. Cut each strip into 8 squares 5" × 5" (12.5 × 12.5 cm) for a total of 32 squares. Cut 1 piece H from each square.

FROM YELLOW PRINT FABRIC:
- Cut 19 strips 4½" (11.5 cm) × WOF. From 11 strips, cut 32 strips 4½" × 12½" (11.5 × 31.5 cm). From 8 strips, cut 32 rectangles 4½" × 8½" (11.5 × 21.5 cm).

the pattern

PETAL
PUSHER
QUILT

the mix
A simple block, twisted and repeated, with a side of curves

Easily the largest quilt in this book, Petal Pusher is a surprisingly quick project. You'll probably want to send this one off to a long-arm quilter for finishing due to its size, but just treat yourself. You'll be so glad you did. This highly graphic quilt revels in repetition and a simple color scheme.

continued on the next page >

- Cut 4 strips 5" (12.5 cm) × Cut each strip into 8 squares 5" × 5" (12.5 × 12.5 cm) for a total of 32 squares. Cut 1 piece H from each square.
- Cut 4 strips 5" (12.5 cm) × WOF. Cut each strip into 8 squares 5" × 5" (12.5 × 12.5 cm) for a total of 32 squares. Cut 1 piece H from each square.

FROM GRAY SOLID FABRIC:
- Cut 8 strips 5" (12.5 cm) × WOF. From each strip, cut 8 squares 5" × 5" (12.5 × 12.5 cm) for a total of 64 squares. Cut 1 piece G from 32 squares.
- Cut 4 strips 5" (12.5 cm) × WOF. Cut each strip into 8 squares 5" × 5" (12.5 × 12.5 cm) for a total of 32 squares. Cut 1 piece H from each square.
- Cut 36 strips 2½" (6.5 cm) × WOF for sashing. From 24 of these strips, cut 24 strips 2½" × 24½" (6.5 × 62 cm). From scraps, cut 9 squares 2½" × 2½" (6.5 × 6.5 cm) for cornerstones. Set aside the remaining 12 strips for borders.

FROM BACKING FABRIC:
- Cut 3 rectangles 114" (290 cm) × WOF.

FROM BINDING FABRIC:
- Cut 11 strips 2½" (6.5 m) × WOF.

MAKING THE BLOCKS

Unfinished block size: 24" × 24" (61 × 61 cm)
This quilt has sixteen blocks.

1. Sew together curved pieces G and H **(fig. 1)** as follows:
   - Sew 32 gray solid pieces G to 32 light blue print pieces H.
   - Sew 32 yellow print pieces G to 32 gray solid pieces H.
   - Sew 32 light blue print pieces G to 32 yellow print pieces H.

   Press seams toward piece H. Trim to 4½" × 4½" (11.5 × 11.5 cm) with a ¼" (6 mm) seam allowance on piece G. You will have a total of ninety-six quarter-circle units.

2. To assemble a block, start with the gray petal block center. Sew two yellow G/gray H units from Step 1 to gray squares 4½" × 4½" (11.5 × 11.5 cm), oriented as shown **(fig. 2)**. Press the seams toward the gray squares. Sew the two pairs together, aligning center seams **(fig. 2)**. Press the seam open.

3. With the gray petal block oriented as shown **(fig. 3)**, sew a yellow rectangle 4½" × 8½" (11.5 × 21.5 cm) to the left and right sides. Press the seams toward the yellow rectangles.

4. Sew two light blue G/yellow H units to yellow strips 4½" × 12½" (11.5 × 31.5 cm) **(fig. 4)**. Press the seams toward the yellow strips.

5. Sew the strips from Step 4 to the top and bottom of the gray petal block center, oriented as shown **(fig. 5)**. Press the seams toward the yellow strips.

6. With the block oriented as shown **(fig. 6)**, sew a light blue strip 4½" × 16½" (11.5 × 42 cm) to the left and right sides. Press the seams toward the light blue strips.

7. Sew two gray G/light blue H units to light blue strips 4½" × 20½" (11.5 × 52 cm) **(fig. 7)**. Press the seams toward the light blue strips.

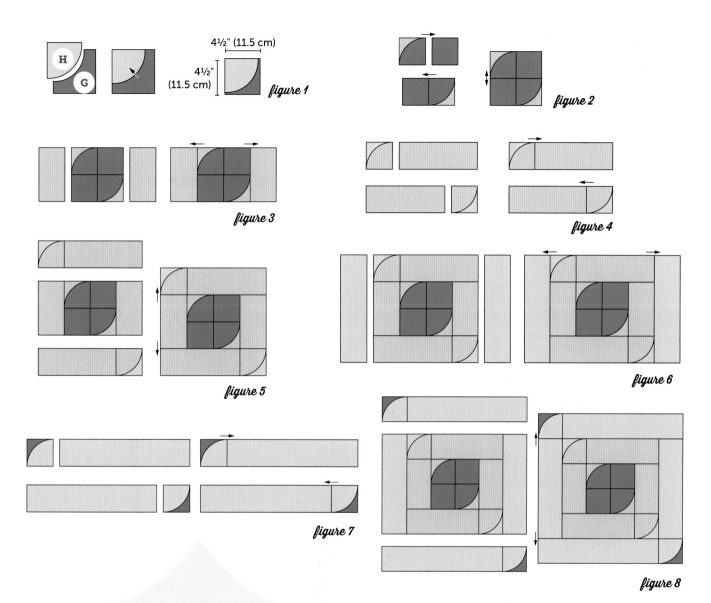

4½" (11.5 cm)

4½" (11.5 cm)

figure 1

figure 2

figure 3

figure 4

figure 5

figure 6

figure 7

figure 8

8 Sew the strips from Step 7 to the top and bottom of the block, oriented as shown **(fig. 8)**. Press the seams toward the light blue strip.

9 Repeat steps 2 through 8 to make a total of sixteen blocks.

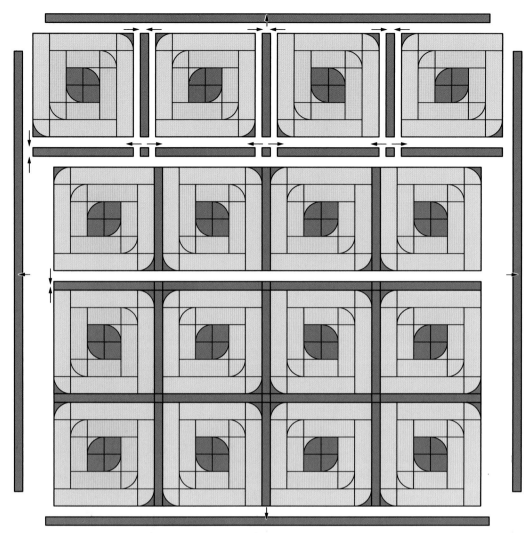

PETAL PUSHER CONSTRUCTION DIAGRAM

MAKING THE QUILT TOP

This quilt has simple squared borders.

1 Refer to the Petal Pusher Construction Diagram to lay out rows 1 and 3, alternating petal directions as shown. . Sew vertical gray sashing strips 2½" x 24½" (6.5 x 62 cm) between the blocks. Press the seams toward the gray strips.

2 Repeat Step 1 for rows 2 and 4, alternating petal directions the opposite way from those in rows 1 and 3, as shown.

3 To make the horizontal sashing rows, alternately sew four gray sashing strips 2½" x 24½" (6.5 x 62 cm) to three gray cornerstone squares 2½" x 2½" (6.5 x 6.5 cm). Make three rows.

4 Sew the block rows and horizontal sashing rows together, aligning adjacent seams. Press seams toward the sashing.

5 To make the borders, sew together four sets of three gray strips 2½" (6.5 cm) x WOF. Trim two long strips to 2½" x 102½" (6.5 x 260 cm) and the other two to

2½" × 106½" (6.5 × 271 cm). Sew the 2½" × 102½" (6.5 × 260 cm) strips to the sides of the quilt. Press the seams toward the borders. Sew the 2½" × 106½" (6.5 × 271 cm) strips to the top and bottom of the quilt. Press the seams toward the borders.

FINISHING

1 Refer to Finishing Your Quilt (page 132) or use your favorite methods to layer and baste the quilt top, batting, and backing.

2 Quilt as desired. Longarm quilter Krista Withers used a concentric swirled circle pantograph design by Patricia Ritter Design.

3 Bind your quilt using my French double-fold binding method as described in Binding (page 139) or your own preferred method.

TIP

- - - - - - - - - - - - - -

Love the pattern but not willing to take on a project this big? Make it in a quarter size for the perfect baby quilt. With a 24" × 24" (61 × 61 cm) block, you can quickly create a 50" × 50" (127 × 127 cm) quilt. Or try eliminating the outer row of each block to reduce the size. You'll still get that great look without the large size!

FINISHING
YOUR QUILT

After you have completed your quilt top, there is still the matter of turning it into an actual quilt. To finish up your beautiful project, you will need to prepare a backing, choose the perfect batting, and layer them together. Then choose your favorite quilting design to quilt together your layers. Finally, bind the edges.

You probably have your own preferred methods and techniques for all these steps in the process. If you're new to quilting, you can consult the many excellent books and websites that describe these basics.

In this section, I share with you my own particular preferences and techniques.

above DETAIL FROM ORANGE TWIST QUILT (PAGE 28)

BACKINGS

Quilt backings are such a personal thing. I know some people who put so much work into their quilt backs that the quilt is essentially two-sided. Others are just grateful to be finished with the quilt top, and they whip together something as quickly as possible.

For the ultimate quick backing, you can use a single length of extra-wide backing fabric (106" to 108" [269 to 274 cm]) but admittedly the choices for these are limited. An alternative—almost as quick—is a backing pieced from standard 42" (106.5 cm) width fabric, pieced with a single seam. This is the option I have used in the yardage requirements for the projects in this book—one long piece of fabric cut in half and seamed together lengthwise.

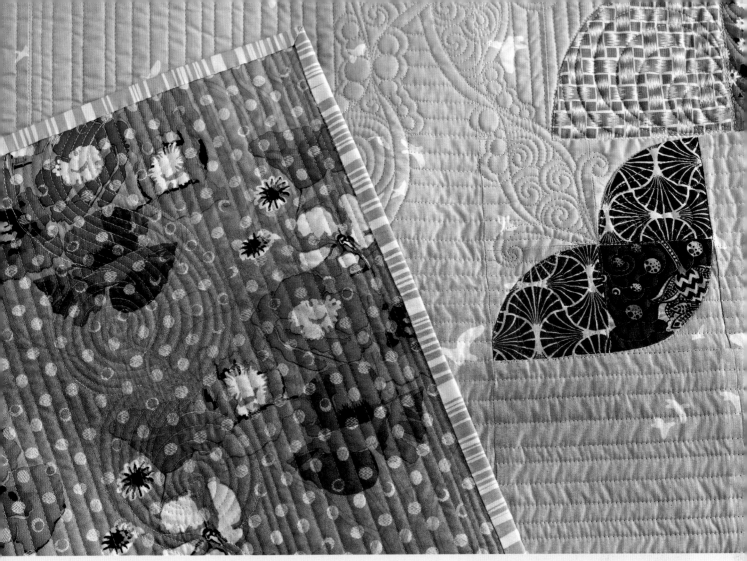

above A FUN, WHIMSICAL FABRIC DRESSES UP THE BACK OF BUTTERFLIES QUILT (PAGE 54).

PIECED OPTIONS

There are a number of pieced backing options that are slightly more complex than a single fabric. I'll admit that I often fall back on these options because I don't have the yardage needed for a large quilt back, which often requires between 5 and 6 yards (4.6 to 5.5 m) of fabric. Using pieced multiple fabrics gives me a chance to use some of those fabrics I've stashed away—those that don't seem to have a home with other fabrics, perhaps because of their color or the scale of the print, and those that make me question why I purchased them in the first place. I can also use those fabrics I just can't bear to chop up.

So, consider these options for your project. Although I don't give you measurements here because they will vary with the project, the following are

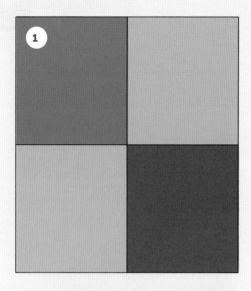

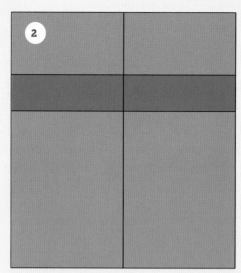

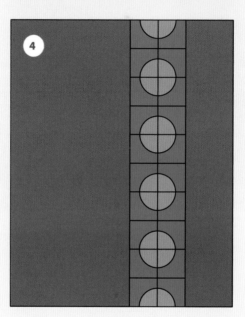

OPTION 1
Four large cuts pieced to meet at the quilt back center.

OPTION 2
A strip pieced horizontally into a single seamed pieced back. This is a useful option when you have a good amount of yardage but not quite enough. It gives you the extra length you need.

OPTION 3
A back composed of fat quarters. I often end up with a collection of fat quarters that I'm not quite sure what to do with. The bonus with these is that they can be from the same fabric line and have a natural cohesion.

OPTION 4
A back that uses up those extra blocks you may have made for the quilt front. Waste not, want not! Put those blocks to good use and enjoy them, even on the back.

a few ideas. You are only limited by your imagination! Backings can be as simple as you like or as creatively complex as you like. It's entirely up to you and your personal preferences.

BATTING

Today, there are choices galore for quilt batting. With a number of manufacturers, the options get better and better all the time. Gone are the days when all quilts were made with polyester high-loft battings (although I personally still have a soft spot for this type of batting). You can choose from cotton, bamboo, soy, polyester, wool, and many combinations of these. There are "green" options for the environmentally minded.

Use the batting you prefer. The quilts in this book are made from all different substrates of batting. My personal preference these days leans strongly toward

left PANTOGRAPH PATTERN BY PATRICIA RITTER DESIGN, QUILTED ON A LONGARM BY KRISTA WITHERS ON PETAL PUSHER QUILT (PAGE 126)

wool. I love the texture it gives and the warmth it provides. (Admittedly, as I write this I'm particularly cold, so it could be coloring my view!)

BASTING

Quilts have traditionally been hand basted or secured with curved safety pins laboriously placed every few inches across the entire quilt. These pins then need to be removed as you quilt the layers. I started with this method and used it successfully to make many quilts. But frankly, I found this to be difficult on my knees and painfully slow. Eventually I made my way to the world of spray basting. And I'll never go back.

Spray basting has made quilting so much easier for me. I've tried a number of brands, and all I can say is that you get what you pay for. If you've tried this method without success, give it a try again with another

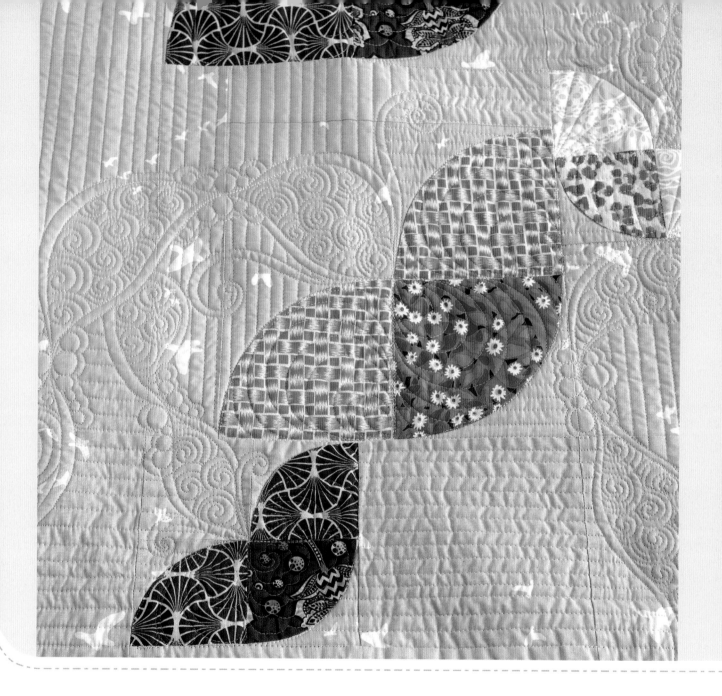

brand. Follow the instructions for proper ventilation, and prepare yourself to be amazed at how quickly you can "baste" a quilt.

QUILTING

For the quilts in this book, I used a combination of quilting techniques. I quilted many of the projects on my domestic sewing machine. Others were quilted by the very talented professional Krista Withers on her longarm machine.

Deciding whether to do the quilting yourself on a domestic machine or to send it to a professional for quilting on a longarm machine is a very personal choice. I love the treat of sending off a large quilt top to a longarm quilter and letting her work her magic on it. It can be expensive, especially for custom work, but it's never a decision that I have regretted. Large quilts,

opposite CUSTOM LONGARM QUILTING BY KRISTA WITHERS ON BUTTERFLIES QUILT (PAGE 54)

right THE AUTHOR USED A STRAIGHT-LINE CROSSHATCH PATTERN TO QUILT ARABIAN NIGHTS QUILT (PAGE 66)

in particular, are much easier to quilt on a longarm machine than on a domestic machine. With longarm quilting, it becomes feasible for most of us to finish the king-sized quilts we all want to make for our own beds. If you go the longarm route, you can choose a custom quilt design and let the talent of your chosen quilter shine. Or you can choose one of the available longarm pantograph designs, which are typically all-over patterns. Make your decision based on what is the right design for your quilt and the style that is most pleasing to you.

Most of us, however—unless we have unlimited funds and/or access to a longarm machine—will be quilting our own quilts on a domestic machine. Although it is outside the scope of this book to offer detailed information about quilting, I'll review the basic choices.

left ON FLOWER POWER QUILT (PAGE 34), THE AUTHOR DID FREE-MOTION QUILTING IN A MEANDERING PATTERN.

Two methods—straight-line quilting and free-motion quilting—are the most commonly used. Simple straight-line quilting, done with a walking foot, is a tried-and-true method that really seems to work with any design, even those with curves. If you are comfortable with straight-line quilting, you can easily do a number of variations, including a crosshatch pattern and a grid.

With free-motion, you can get fancier. The idea of this technique, in which you drop your machine's feed dogs and move the quilt freely under a darning foot, is often frightening to those who haven't tried it. Yet many quilters wind up converting to it almost exclusively, because ultimately it can be a very quick method for finishing up your quilt. The options for free-motion quilting designs are too numerous to list, but basics are a simple meander stitch, spiral stitching, and loops.

There is one additional option for quilting if you have a machine with decorative stitches: use an expanded version of a simple decorative stitch. You can create waves or curves with even a simple zigzag stitch if you "max out" on stitch length and width. Play with the stitch options on your machine to see what is available, and think outside the box!

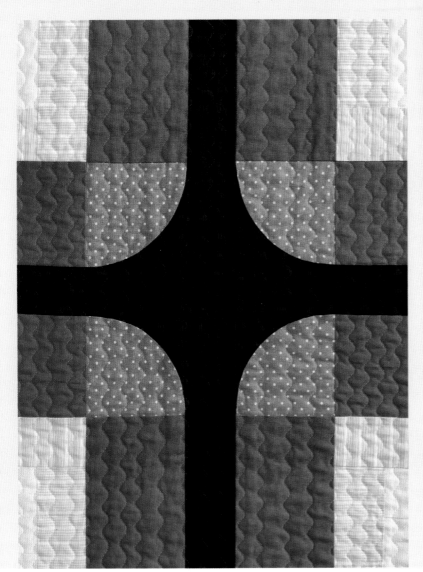

left TENNIS MATCH QUILT (PAGE 48) WAS
QUILTED BY THE AUTHOR USING A BASIC
ZIGZAG STITCH SET LONG AND WIDE.

above BINDING ON NINE PATCH CURVES
QUILT (PAGE 84)

BINDING

Binding is the final step in completing your quilt. It is
personally one of my favorite moments with my quilt.
(Let the stoning begin!) I use a French double-fold
binding method that is machine sewn to the front and
handsewn to the back. I love the perfect finish I get with
this, and I enjoy the time spent with the quilt at the very
end. I work my way around the quilt one stitch at a time,
touching each edge of the quilt for one last time.

To make the binding, first cut the necessary
number of strips 2½" (6.5 cm) × WOF. You will find this
number in the cutting list for each project in this book.
You can cut all these strips from one fabric, or create
a scrappy binding by using multiple fabrics. (This is a
great way to add to your fabric if you don't have quite
enough for the binding.) If you so choose, you may
cut these strips on the bias for a bias binding. I usually
don't bother with a bias binding unless I will be binding
a curved edge.

figure 1

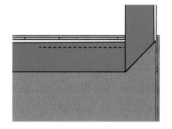

5" (12.5 cm)

¼" (6 mm)

figure 2

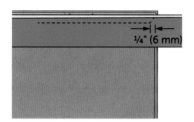

¼" (6 mm)

figure 3

figure 4

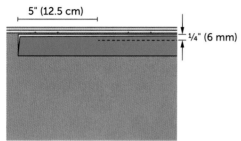

figure 5

MAKING A FRENCH DOUBLE-FOLD BINDING

1 Sew the strips together using diagonal seams to create one long strip of fabric (**fig. 1**). Place the ends of two strips perpendicular, right sides together. Sew a diagonal seam from the upper left corner to the bottom right corner. Trim away the excess fabric to leave a ¼" (6 mm) seam allowance. Press the seam open.

2 Fold the binding strip wrong sides together along the length, and press.

3 To sew the binding to the quilt, place the binding strip on the quilt top, aligning the binding strip raw edges with the quilt edge. Do not start in a corner, but rather in the middle of one side. Leave a 5" (12.5 cm) tail unsewn at the beginning of the binding (**fig. 2**). Stitch the binding to the quilt using a generous ¼" (6 mm) seam allowance.

4 When you near a corner of the quilt, stop stitching ¼" (6 mm) from the end (**fig. 3**). Turn the quilt, and stitch the binding at a 45-degree angle to the corner.

5 Remove the quilt from the machine, and fold back the binding along the diagonal stitching, aligning the raw edges of the binding with the raw edge of the quilt (**fig. 4**).

6 Fold the binding back down, matching the folded edge of the binding with the quilt top (**fig. 5**). Continue sewing along the edge of the quilt. Repeat steps 4 through 6 for all corners.

7 As you near the end of the binding and approach the tail you left at the beginning, stop stitching about 10" (25.5 cm) from the initial stitches.

8 Trim the binding so that the edges of the first tail overlap the end tail by 2½" (6.5 cm) (**fig. 6**).

9 Open the binding tails and lay the fabrics right sides together, placing the beginning tail end over the ending tail end, just as you did to piece the strips together. Pin. You will most likely need to squish the quilt together under the binding as you work. Don't be afraid to do this. Sew a diagonal seam from the upper left-hand corner to the bottom right-hand corner as shown (**fig. 7**).

10. Trim the excess fabric leaving a ¼" (6 mm) seam allowance. Press the seam open. Fold the binding back in half, wrong sides together, and stitch it in place along the edge of the quilt.

11. Flip the folded edge of the binding to the back of the quilt and hold it in place with spring clips such as Clover Wonder Clips. With a needle and thread, handsew the binding in place, using a small, hidden stitch.

12. To miter the corners of the binding, first fold the binding along the stitched edge and hand crease an angle into the binding (fig. 8).

13. Fold the angled, folded edge of the binding back over the corner, and handstitch it in place (fig. 9). Continue stitching around the entire quilt perimeter.

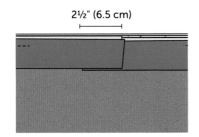

figure 6

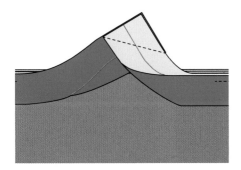

figure 7

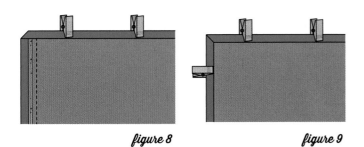

figure 8   figure 9

template pattern guide

note Some template patterns are oversized compared to the finished dimensions to allow for trimming the finished block to size. Note the gray trim lines on some patterns for the modern block pieces.

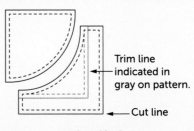

Trim line indicated in gray on pattern.

Cut line

modern block

project name	page #	templates
ORANGE TWIST QUILT	28	I, J, U, V
FLOWER POWER QUILT	34	A, B, E, F
PAIR OF PILLOWS	40	A, B
TENNIS MATCH QUILT	48	A, B, G, H
BUTTERFLIES QUILT	54	M, N, Y, Z, W, X
MEDALLION BABY QUILT	62	E, F
ARABIAN NIGHTS QUILT	66	C, D
TELEPORT QUILT	72	Y, Z
NINE PATCH CURVES QUILT	84	K, L
LOOSELY CURVED WALL HANGING	92	A, B
PAINT DRIPS QUILT	98	M, N, O, P
MOD GARDEN LAP QUILT	106	G, H
ORNAMENTAL QUILT	114	G, H, Q, R
SUNRISE TABLE RUNNER	120	G, H
PETAL PUSHER QUILT	126	G, H

RESOURCES

DIE-CUTTERS AND TOOLS

AccuQuilt
accuquilt.com

Fiskars
fiskars.com

Just Curves (special foot, acrylic curve templates, etc.)
justcurves.biz

Sizzix
sizzix.com

FABRIC AND THREAD

SOME OF MY FAVORITE FABRICS AND THREAD COME FROM THESE MANUFACTURERS.

Art Gallery Fabrics
artgalleryfabrics.com

Aurifil (thread)
www.aurifil.com

Birch Fabrics
birchfabrics.com

Cloud9 Fabrics
cloud9fabrics.com

Dear Stella
dearstelladesign.com

Free Spirit Fabrics
freespiritfabric.blogspot.com

Michael Miller Fabrics
michaelmillerfabrics.com

Moda Fabrics
unitednotions.com

Oakshott Fabrics
www.oakshottfabrics.com

Pellon (batting and pillow forms)
shoppellon.com

Robert Kaufman Fabrics
robertkaufman.com

LONGARM QUILTING SERVICES

Krista Withers Quilting
kristawithersquilting.blogspot.com

INDEX

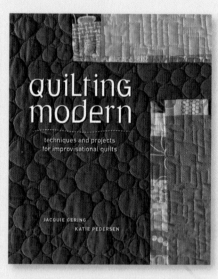